GLORY IN TH

'This is a timely book. Worship and music play a huge part in the life of the church. It is important that we catch the heart of Jarrod's message. God is seeking true worshippers. We must guard against simply becoming "consumers" of the latest worship styles, songs and music.'

Noel Richards, worship leader and songwriter

'The word radical has often been overstated and even misused. This book is truly radical in the sense that it exhorts a returning to essential basic principles. A re-discovery of a true heart of worship and praise is a "now" message and one that has been skilfully presented by Jarrod Cooper. This book is truly passionate and dangerous. I warmly commend it.'

Chris Bowater, songwriter and worship leader

'This excellent book by Jarrod issues a challenge to those who have encamped around the outward form of contemporary worship as an end in itself and encourages us all to pursue a higher call of experiencing the tangible presence of God in our lives, homes, and church gatherings.'

Dave Bilbrough, songwriter and worship leader

'Corporate and individual worship, songs and worship leaders are relevant subjects for the twenty-first-century church. Jarrod addresses these necessary aspects with wisdom, practicality and in the context of the glory of God. Jarrod is also a practitioner of the principles he writes about. This book is essential reading for all who want to worship God in spirit and in truth.'

Paul C. Weaver, General Superintendent of the Assemblies of God in Great Britain and Ireland

'A worship book with a difference! Taking you from singing mere songs, to a lifestyle of worship! True to his own life of worship, Jarrod writes with tremendous balance and revelation of that which has become a lifestyle to him – worship in spirit and truth. Reading this book will not only change your life but will lead you into a new dimension.'

Suzette Hattingh, Director, Voice in the City

'In this honest and challenging book, Jarrod both takes us back to the basics of worship and points us towards new frontiers in the pursuit of God's glory. It is deeply spiritual, highly practical, and I hope it will be made widely available.'

Stuart Bell, Leader of the New Life Christian Fellowship, Lincoln

'*Glory in the Church* is a valuable contribution towards the new move of worship which is beginning to sweep God's church, focusing people on what it really means to glorify the King enthroned on high. It is time to take our eyes off ourselves and worship him!'

Colin Urquhart, pastor and founder, Kingdom Faith

'God has promised, as surely as he lives to fill the earth with his glory (Hab. 2:14). For this to happen we must see his glory fill the church. Jarrod leaves no stone unturned as he seeks, through the word and God's dealings with him, to teach, inspire and enlighten us in how to move as pilgrims towards the fulfilment of the promise.'

David Hadden, worship leader and songwriter

GLORY IN THE CHURCH

A fresh blueprint for worship in the 21st Century

Jarrod Cooper

Authentic

LONDON ● COLORADO SPRINGS ● HYDERABAD

This edition published 2008 by Authentic Media
9 Holdom Avenue, Bletchley, Milton Keynes, MK1 1QR, UK
1820 Jet Stream Drive, Colorado Springs, CO 80921, USA
OM Authentic Media, Medchal Road, Jeedimetla Village,
Secunderabad 500 055, A.P., India
www.authenticmedia.co.uk

Authentic Media is a division of IBS-STL U.K., limited by guarantee, with its
Registered Office at Kingstown Broadway, Carlisle, Cumbria, CA3 0HA.
Registered in England & Wales No. 1216232. Registered charity 270162

British Library Cataloguing in Publication Data
A catalogue record for this book is available from the British Library

ISBN-13: 978-1-86024-623-4

Cover Design by David Lund
Print Management by Adare Carwin
Printed in Great Britain by J.H. Haynes & Co., Sparkford

ACKNOWLEDGEMENTS

Huge thanks go to my wonderful wife Vicky, 'the one he kept for me'. I love you with all my heart. This, my first book, is dedicated to you. May the adventure of the glory and presence of God outlined in these pages be the reality of our whole lifetime together.

Special thanks also go to Gerald Coates for a wonderful foreword. You are an outstanding spiritual father to so many. Thank you for all you have done for the church in our nation. Thanks also to my parents David and Marion Cooper and to my brother Jason; to Paul, Lis, Joel and Alex Gutteridge, and Rob and Janette Saggs, who all work so hard with me in this adventure. Also to Andrew and Lynn Widdowson, to all at the New Life Christian Centre in Hull, and to so many other people who have worked endlessly with me. Thanks, too, to pastors around the UK and abroad who have put up with my ministry, who have been agitated, inspired and irritated, and yet have responded so graciously to my expressions of longing for the Father's glory to impact our world. I honour and love you.

My greatest thanks to my God, and to Jesus Christ his Son.

Contents

FOREWORD

So – have we replaced God's glory with our programmes? If we have, is there anything we can do to get
the glory of God back into our gatherings and into individual lives? What exactly is the glory of God? These are
the issues Jarrod Cooper puts to us in an often challenging and provocative fashion, whilst providing plenty of
biblical evidence and illustrations to support his concerns.

What we do have, he contends, is good music, well-
written songs, sufficient time slots to fill and a history to
learn from. But does God's presence, his glory, fill our
gatherings as it did in Old Testament times and indeed
New Testament times? And if the presence of God is not
with us when we gather in homes or in public buildings,
how can we go forward?

Most of the book has to do with meetings and gatherings of the assembled church. In a post-modern world that
may be surprising. But I do not know of a church that is
effective in seeing the lost found, those in darkness living
in the light and the unredeemed thoroughly saved without it being gathered to the word, the presence and the
glory of God. It is clear from the New Testament that the
church was both gathered and scattered at the same time.

Even in seasons of intense persecution, when the church was scattered because of religious or military oppression, they still endeavoured to gather privately, underground, to worship and pray, to fellowship and eat together.

The scattered church without the gathered church will produce people primarily interested in their own lives, ministries, agendas and culture. This militates against the genius of the body of Christ, where racism, sexism and nationalism as well as ageism (whether it be youth culture or the elderly) and individualism are dealt with through a Gospel which is all-inclusive.

That is not to say that there is no room for different cultural expressions of church, whether it be among the young, the elderly, ethnic minorities or those with a particular taste in music. But it becomes exclusive and self-satisfying unless right at the heart of it there is a desire to win the lost and a strategy in place to do that, which might initially be more attractive to a particular culture than the broad three-generational, multicultural church gathering (which sadly is usually one culture anyway).

So there are many challenges ahead, whether or not we read this book or agree with the writer's perspectives. My experience is that even when a gathering is not to someone's cultural taste, if the presence of the glory of God is at the heart of the event, cultural preferences get laid aside for something much more meaningful. I once took a group of teenage women and men from one of our Pioneer churches who were struggling with the culture of 'the meeting' to a black church where I was speaking. The style of music and worship and the songs themselves were completely alien, but they knelt, wept and stood with arms outstretched because they touched the presence of the glory of God.

Is it possible that there is only a song in our hearts when there is a microphone, worship leader and overhead projector present? Or have we become religious? Religion has little to do with hassocks and cassocks, robes and dog collars. All of that can be part of a religious front. But on one occasion God told people that the issue was their hearts, not their garments. No, religion is much deeper than one's apparel. Religion is doing God things (worship, prayer, Bible reading, affectionate greeting) at God times, in God places. But if we rarely open our Bibles outside of the gathering setting, rarely sing God's praises without the aforementioned paraphernalia, and treat people one way outside of Christian events and another way in them, we have become religious. We are, as I say, doing God things at God times at God places, which may well be the local parish church, but could be the local school hall.

This is what Jarrod Cooper is consumed with, carrying the presence and glory of God in life and not just in meetings. But if there is no glory when we meet in the twos and threes or with two or three hundred, it is unlikely we will carry the presence and glory of God to school, in the workplace, at home or in our social lives.

If you want to see the glory of God recovered in your life, among your friends and in the church, be prepared to lay down or deal with anything that may hinder the presence of God and his glory pervading who you are and what you do.

John, Jesus' best friend, spoke so eloquently about the glory that was Jesus that nobody has ever improved upon it. 'The Word became flesh and blood, and moved into the neighbourhood. We saw the glory with our own eyes, the one-of-a kind glory, like Father, like Son, generous inside and out, true from start to finish' (John 1:14, *The Message*).

And whilst I don't believe John's words can be improved upon, the Apostle Paul did rather well when he wrote:

Glory to God in the church!
Glory to God in the Messiah, in Jesus!
Glory down all the generations!
Glory through all millennia! Oh, yes!
(*Eph. 3:21*, The Message)

Gerald Coates, speaker,
author and broadcaster

INTRODUCTION

Today was the day my worship ministry would change forever and I didn't even know it.

I woke at 6.30am to the sounds of zebra and warthogs munching stubs of grass in the garden outside. Peering wearily across the African plain from our lodge, I suddenly remembered we were due at Rita's morning prayer meeting in just a few minutes. I downed a coffee and splashed my face, then clambered aboard the pickup truck and we headed off to the meeting on the dusty earth road to Rita's dairy farm.

Rita was an extraordinary prophetess. The moment I met her she told me all about myself with such grace and humility, you couldn't be fearful of her 'finding things out', as she would only love you anyway. She lived in bush land here in the northern reaches of southern Africa with five hundred workers under her care. She had raised the dead and prophesied to governments, and she often took witch doctors onto her workforce, having proved that Jesus' power was greater than theirs – a spectacle that led to many wide-eyed hours around the dinner table, drinking in stories usually attributed to scriptural heroes and other dead folk.

As a young white girl in southern Africa, Rita had been institutionalised because of her love for the black people and because she spoke in tongues. Ostracised from the established church, she found herself learning directly from God, reading the Bible and simply believing it. The results terrified the religious but met the needs of the hurting and lonely. She grew up to become an extraordinary figure.

As our pick-up truck neared the meeting place, sounds of African singing bustled through the passing air, along with the rhythmic thunder of several hundred feet pounding the ground in praise. Turning through the gate of her dairy farm, there in the fresh African sun, we were met by a huge circle of smiling, worshipping faces, raising high praise to a God who was the same the world over. There, in the centre of the circle, Rita span and danced, her curly blonde hair bouncing over her skinny frame as she led her church in praise and prayer, the red dust bursting upwards from under the dancing feet. At a meeting like this only weeks before, the ground had shaken violently as they prayed, just as in the book of Acts. I was ready for anything to happen!

The singing went on, and various members of our team shared with the grateful congregation gathered. I knew soon the finger would be pointed at me and Rita would ask me to step forward. Nervously I thought of what I could say. What would be relevant out here, where they see more of God's power on a weekly basis than my whole network of friends and ministries see in a year? Here was a living, breathing equivalent of Smith Wigglesworth and Kathryn Kuhlman rolled into one. What could I possibly say? Eventually she turned, pointed her finger at me lovingly and asked me the last thing I hoped she would ever ask: 'Come and lead us in worship.'

Terror gripped me, I mumbled something about not feeling up to it (I led hundreds in worship weekly back home!) and hid behind the person next to me. Kindly she didn't make an issue of it and moved on. And yet something had hit me, and where Rita didn't press her point, God began to.

Why is it that I felt I couldn't lead worship out here? Why did I feel restricted, useless and out of place? Why was it that my God in Britain, the God of my meetings and ministry, seemed distant here in Africa? Slowly, as the days went on, I realised that I was trapped in a blueprint that revolved around my western culture and had little to do with God. To me, church had to do with overhead slides and video projectors, microphones and instruments. Worship times that lasted a certain length, involved the latest songs, and in which I had learnt (quite skilfully, if I may say so) to play along to people singing in tongues – until they got bored and wanted another song, that is.

My blueprint for church and worship involved platforms, tuneful singing, rows of seats and a room full of spectators. Now, stepping outside of my blueprint, I suddenly realised how impotent my ministry was. It wasn't based on God, his calling, my hearing of his voice and obedience. It wasn't accredited by his power in signs and wonders. It was based on imitation, conformity to a western Christian culture and the expectations of the crowd. God wasn't readily available in his power. In reality he had to move within certain boundaries and cultural expectations. Perhaps that's why I had never experienced the dead raised, the ground shaken, or governments enlisting my opinions.

Something began to stir in me. I felt like a fake. I felt like my church was a fake. Just one small glimpse of God in a foreign culture and I realised how much I had interpreted

God through my own Christian customs and traditions. Did I know God? I knew the God of the Baptists, Methodists, Anglicans, Pentecostals, charismatics, house churches and many others, but did I know God? I was challenged to the core.

On reflection, the truth is that I had felt like a fake for a long time! I had read the book of Acts and looked at my church and life, and felt utterly hypocritical. I longed for his glory to move among us, but something inside me was telling me that my powerlessness was more my fault than his. Rather like the disciples who fell asleep in the cloud of God's glory in Luke 9, only just waking in time to see Jesus transfigured in all his splendour, it was more about my need to wake up to his glory than whether or not he was willing to manifest his power.

Indeed, this day had become a wake-up call for me. But could I now stir from my comfortable cultural slumber to find the glory of God? Could I move beyond my apathetic western pattern of worship and find the purity of God's presence and will, outside of time, fashion and custom? Could I walk away from years of politely serving the God of the British and find the God of all glory? Something told me that if I could, then I would stand in the place where all true giants of God have stood. The very place where the power of heaven can pierce our culture and impact the earth in revival and reformation.

This book begins with my own story of stepping outside my education and experience to meet with a God ready to touch our lives and fill our churches with glory. It is a story of frustration, of seeking and of occasionally finding. It gives no quick fixes, no magic formulas, and if read correctly it may even leave you with more questions than when you started. But in asking questions, as I did on that life-changing day in the African bush, I believe we take a step beyond what has been, into what could be. It seems the more I journey, the more questions arise. But then again, there has never been a revival or reformation without questions. Questions have always been the early heralds of a dawning move of God.

PART 1

A BLUEPRINT FOR CORPORATE WORSHIP

Visions of glory fill my mind
Footprints of ancient saints I find
Leaving their passions, once they climbed
To be lost in your glory.

Chapter 1

AN ERA OF GLORY IS COMING

Longing, dreaming, for more than this
Hoping, hurting, I crave your kiss
Upon my life, upon my land
Upon my feeble human plans
I dream, I ask . . .
Would you come and rest your glory on my life?

Moses had risen early that morning and set out on the long journey up Mount Sinai, as God had commanded. Just the day before, he had asked God: 'Show me your glory.' God had responded: 'I will cause all my goodness to pass in front of you' and had sent him up the mountain for an encounter with his glory.

After the gruelling ascent, Moses settled on a rock, high on the peak of the lonely mountain. Standing, prayerfully, he meditated on God's goodness and waited for him to arrive. He didn't know what would happen. He just knew something would.

As his heart calmed from the climb and his breathing steadied, he began to focus on the details of the panoramic view surrounding him. He saw other mountain peaks and plains, and he could just hear the bustle of the nomadic community of Israel going about their business in the valley below. Then he noticed something beginning to appear in the sky far off to the east, moving slowly closer. Faint at first, like whispering winds, then stronger, thicker and deeper, an advancing cloud, dark yet pure, slowly began to fill the air around him. Spellbound, he stood transfixed until he was completely engulfed by the mysterious mist. Then, just as the cloud had grown so thick as to completely obscure his view, a blazing light burst through the darkness, blinding his eyes with brightness.

Fear, excitement and awe flooded Moses all at once and, in an instant, he was picked up and thrust by an invisible hand into a man-sized hole in the rock. Slowly turning and peeking from behind the boulder, he stared, lost in the moment, watching the unfolding beauty of the supernatural unveiling itself in the natural. God had come.

Just when it seemed his senses could take no more mystery, a voice pierced the cloud and light. A voice that was like a man's, like rivers, like the cry of an eagle and the blast of a trumpet all at once. Then he saw him. The Creator. God walking, as he had done before history began, in the cool of the day with his first friend-man, Adam.

'The Lord, the Lord, the compassionate and gracious God, slow to anger, abounding in love and faithfulness,' the voice proclaimed.

Moses' every cell dissolved at the impact of the voice – emotion, mind, will and body weakened at the words. Bowing to the ground, he worshipped with the worship of a man humbled, yet honoured. Broken, yet made. Moses had met the glory of God.

There are moments when God steps from the invisible into the visible. Moments when God, who is so often hidden and working behind the scenes and in realms we fail to understand, leaps into the view of our human frailty and makes himself so obvious that no one can deny it.

Moments when we see water turned to wine, broken lives healed, people shining like lightning, fire bursting from heaven and the dead raised back to life. These are moments when 'all God's goodness passes in front of us'. When his greatness is revealed to our eyes, ears and feelings. Not God hidden, not God being subtle, but God impacting our human senses.

These moments are called 'the glory of God'.

Longing for Glory

My own journey to know God's glory began when I realised the difference between a temple filled with his glory and a church service filled with human plans and programmes.

I had been ministering for several days at a large conference, where, to be honest, not a lot had happened. It was the third day of the event and I was invited to lead worship, a task I wasn't relishing as the people were about as fired up as a damp fish!

As I stood on the platform that night, in desperation I asked God what to do. He told me to sing a quiet little song, and I dutifully did – eyes firmly shut, as it was too discouraging to open them! After I'd sung the song, God asked me to invite the Holy Spirit to come amongst us. We did, and to my utter surprise people began to fall down, all around the meeting place, under the power of the Spirit. For three hours the glory of God invaded the meeting. The preacher didn't get to preach, the worship group didn't really sing too many songs, and those with demonic problems ran out of the service, only to be delivered by an evangelist in the cafeteria next door! It was a glorious outpouring of God.

Something moved deep in my heart that night. I knew I'd found something in God that suddenly made sense. It went beyond music, beyond singing, beyond me scheduling a nice little meeting. It was God himself, invading his own church and being the glory among us. Ever since then, all I have wanted to do is build a ministry, temple, lifestyle and church where God's glory can dwell.

I quickly learned that in order for me to do that, he had to overwhelm much that I had previously admired and called 'church'. He had to show me his blueprint for a glory-filled temple.

An Apostolic Reformation Will Lead to Glory

Over the past century, God has been reforming many great ministries and truths in the church across the world. We have seen reformations of the Holy Spirit and his gifts of healing, tongues, faith and prophecy. We have seen the restoration of true biblical offices in the church, with great evangelists and teachers raised up. More recently we have seen the worldwide recognition and acceptance of prophets, a foundational ministry giving eyes and insight to the church.

Finally, over the past couple of decades, and with increasing intensity, God has been restoring the office of the apostle to the church. Just like the prophet, the apostle is a foundational ministry, Ephesians 2:20 states that the church is 'built on the foundation of the apostles and prophets'. The function of apostolic ministry, in short, is to father, plant, build and oversee the church, and to bring God's order and structure to it. The restoration of apostolic ministry excites me more than that of any other ministry, because it means that the temple of the church is being built into an ordered structure. This, I believe, will precede a visitation of God's glory in the earth in a measure previously unseen.

God's Blueprint Brings God's Glory

Imagine Solomon building the temple in Jerusalem, or Moses erecting the tabernacle in the desert. They found God's blueprint and built what he asked of them. This is an apostolic role. They gathered all the materials, used all the skills in the people around them, and built a wonderful temple for God. When it was finished and everything was in place, just as God had designed, he came in all his glory and filled the temple! This infilling or habitation was God's acceptance and approval of what had been built. He came to dwell among his people in power and splendour. God is still looking for a temple to call 'home'.

Today we, the church, are the temple of God, being 'built together to become a dwelling in which God lives' (Eph. 2:22). The rise of apostolic ministries means that all the gifting and people are ready to be built together as a beautiful temple for God. As each of us finds our function in this divine, dynamic, mobile temple called the church, his glory will invade us just as it invaded Solomon and Moses.

This apostolic era, then, is the forerunner, herald and announcer of an age of glory. An era of infilling. An era of the intensity of God poured out among us, so that the church may become 'the fullness of him' as Paul describes us in Ephesians 1:23. Can you sense the creaking of heaven's gates and the brooding of his power over churches today, as apostolic ministries set in place the temple of God? Can you sense the groaning of heaven and the longing of the earth (Rom. 8:19), as God is about to sweep into our world with all his glory upon the church? It will be said of us, 'The glory of the Lord has risen upon you' (Is. 60:1). Now is the time to build a temple according to the divine blueprint of heaven and for us to present ourselves ready for his coming.

Can He Overwhelm You and Your Plans?

But apostolic reformation, redesigning and preparing the church for an age of God's glory among us, will not come without cost. It will take a special kind of people who are willing for God to overwhelm their plans and programmes, their learning and culture.

I was recently invited to minister in song at a conference in Mexico, where several thousand leaders from Central America were present. It was a glorious time with God moving powerfully in meeting after meeting.

One very special event occurred that touched my heart. Each night thirty dancers streamed out of the side doors into the front of the arena: a mass of flags, exuberance and excitement, raising a glorious noise of colour to God in praise. It was wonderful.

What touched me most is that every night these thirty worshippers would dance, perfectly choreographed and obviously well practised, but within forty minutes every dancer would have stumbled to the floor under the power of the Spirit. Laughing, crying, worshipping and praying, they lay overwhelmed by God each evening.

In much the same way, we are on a journey of discovery, seeking a blueprint from heaven that may overwhelm our well-practised plans and long-held worship culture. Church is not ultimately the place for our performances, sermons or tastes. It should be the place that God will so enjoy that he himself will dance into our auditoriums, filling and thrilling us with the acceptance of our worship by the manifestation of his presence.

Are you willing to think hard with me about our blueprint for worship? Are you willing to ask some terrifyingly honest questions about worship culture today? Most importantly, are you willing to change your culture, should God speak to you at any time as you read the pages of this book? Could you, like my Mexican friends, fall metaphorically overwhelmed by heaven's advances, even if your culture of worship is well-practised and has cost you dearly over the years?

If you are, then you are ready to read on.

The Challenge of the Chapter

- The glory of God is God revealed to our senses.
- Do you want to go beyond song singing, to discover the glory of God?
- The rise of apostles means God is building his temple, the church.
- God wants to fill the temple with his glory.
- Can God overwhelm your plans with his glory?

Chapter 2

FRUSTRATION FROM HEAVEN

I've seen your eyes, empty and tired
Longing for something to rekindle the ancient fires
Of all you once desired
But look at your feet, pampered and soft
They haven't climbed to any mountain tops
In a long, long while
No wonder it's hard to smile . . .

A recent survey revealed that 'a majority of people leave church without feeling that they experienced God's presence' and that 'in a typical weekend, less than one-third of adults who attend services feel as if they truly interacted with God.'

As I travel ministering, my personal feeling is that thousands of sincere, God-fearing individuals are longing for so much more in worship. As I speak messages like those outlined in this book, many worship leaders, musicians and worshippers agree that they are longing to go beyond the shallowness of our current corporate gatherings. They have a deep gut-feeling that we are missing God with our current culture and design for corporate worship.

Despite the current hype on the Christian music scene, the rise in worship albums, famous worship leaders and concert-type events, there are three signs in the world of local church worship that are causing a whisper of frustration in those who desire God's Spirit and glory to move among us.

The First Sign: Predictability

The first sign is that I can tell you almost exactly what is going to happen at your church next Sunday. You'll start with three fast songs, move into four slow songs, followed by communion, then the 'word' and, if you're a really spiritual church, you'll end with a ministry time. Okay, that may not be exactly the pattern for some, but whatever your particular stream or style, most will admit predictability pervades our programmes.

In John 3:8 Jesus says: 'The wind blows wherever it pleases. You hear its sound, but you cannot tell where it comes from or where it is going. So it is with everyone born of the Spirit.'

You cannot tell where a person of the Spirit is going. He or she is as unpredictable as the wind. But amazingly we know exactly where most leaders will go next during a service. Most congregation members can pre-empt their leader's moves. They sit down ready for communion. They fidget when it's time for the message to end!

If John 3:8 is true, we have to ask the honest question: Are we calling things 'spiritual' that are not of God? Is it God telling us to meet for one-and-a-half hours each week and churn out this liturgical offering to him? Is it true to say that God, whose imagination designed both the flea and the elephant, the buttercup and the oak, can only think up this ritualistic, predictable singing of songs, week after week, around the globe? Or have we perhaps become victims of our own westernised, Christian culture? Are we simply doing what was done before us? Are we truly a temple for his glory, or have we become a well-planned song and sermon machine?

The Second Sign: Prayerlessness

I regularly ask congregations where I minister, 'How many of you struggle with your prayer life?' In most churches, in the dozen or more countries I have visited, 95 per cent of the members slip up their hands and admit: 'I struggle to pray.'

This presents us with a problem. If Brother Cho and every other revivalist are correct, and prayer really is the key to revival, there is an issue that needs addressing: What are we doing, or not doing, that is making prayer so difficult? We have endless books and conferences on prayer, but is there something more foundational that we have overlooked? This prayerlessness is the second sign of our need for a new blueprint.

The Third Sign: Worship Leader Dependency

On my travels, many pastors tell me that the worship at their church is great. Being slightly mischievous, I'm tempted to ask: 'Take away your music group and ask your people to worship. That's how good your worship really is.' I usually give in to the temptation!

Many churches lose a few talented musicians and suddenly realise how worshipless their congregation is. Behind the façade of 'holy' faces, most were actually just singing along to the music rather than interacting with God.

Pastors are under so much pressure to have a great band of musicians in their church that if the devil's brother-in-law walked in the door and was able to play guitar, they'd stick him behind a microphone and have him leading their corporate celebrations! A slight exaggeration perhaps, but closer to the truth than it's comfortable to admit.

Have we become so dependent on music rather than mature Christianity and Spirit-filled leadership that we have bred a weak, entertainment-orientated version of Christianity?

Frustration Comes From Heaven

These and other signs were apparent through my own early years of worship-leading in the 1980s and early 1990s. Numerous questions brought enough frustration to my life to cause me to step out on a journey seeking more.

Could there possibly be more to worship than the 'few fast songs, few slow songs' worship time? Is there some way we can go beyond this current culture of worship, a design that, apart from some new songs, seems little changed since the 1970s? Is it possible for the church of God to become a place of prayer and power? Can we really be overwhelmed by the power and glory of God week after week? Can we get back to the expectancy that anything can (and indeed will) happen when we meet together? Surely we cannot expect such fervour and devotion in a western culture? Or can we?

The Challenge of the Chapter

- Most people leave church feeling they have not experienced God's presence.
- Are your church meetings predictable?
- Do you struggle to pray?
- Do only a small percentage of your church turn up to prayer meetings?
- Do you only worship when musicians or worship leaders are helping you?

Chapter 3

SEARCHING FOR A NEW BLUEPRINT

Take the hand of God, climb a mountainside
See the Promised Land, let it fill your eyes
Light a raging fire that consumes your fears
Have you been dreaming?
It's time you were gazing
Through the eyes of God.

The Misuse of the Music Ministry

In 1993 I was a worship leader and elder at a church of a hundred or so people in East Yorkshire. Seeing the signs of weakness mentioned in the previous chapter, my minister and I discussed at length possible solutions. My response was simple, if a little radical. I believed the solution for us lay in re-evaluating our use of the music ministry and in re-establishing a true following of the Spirit during our meetings. We had to remove the musicians for a time and learn to be church without them.

I remember, as if it was yesterday, teaching for the very first time on the misuse of the music ministry and weaknesses in worship. I expressed my desire to truly follow the Holy Spirit and to see a church full of mature, prayerful, pro-active members. I presented to our church all the signs of weakness we had identified and went on to establish that when the following things happen, we are at risk of ignoring God's blueprint for local church.

When Songs Replace Prayer

When we replace the New Testament dynamic of corporate prayer with music and the singing of songs, we turn our local churches from powerhouses to theatre houses. Only spectators go to theatres. Songs are great and biblical, but they have so overwhelmed the God-ordained centrality of prayer that our churches have lost the ability to pray.

When we hide prayer in a side-room meeting and give out specialist tags to intercessors, we take prayer out of the church and make it the tool of just a few. That's why most Christians can't pray at home. They never learn in church what they need in order to pray at home. All that most congregations do in church is sing songs and listen to sermons!

When Ritual Replaces Relationship

When we replace following the Spirit and listening to God's voice (as Jesus taught) with ritualistic meetings, we sink into powerless religion. God is alive and wants to lead our meetings by the guidance of his Holy Spirit. That will make us as unpredictable as the wind (Jn. 3:8) and take us beyond the 'fast song, slow song' worship formula currently followed by most churches.

When Entertainment Replaces Cost

Some leaders worry about making our main church services too challenging for most of the church. But Jesus didn't worry about being 'seeker-friendly'. He spat, made mud packs, got angry and preached sermons many people didn't understand! His Spirit's outpouring was marked by people appearing drunk and babbling in tongues. His early church featured confrontational preaching, power that brought fear to cities and prayer that was loud and passionate.

Maybe if we took prayer and other less palatable activities right into the centre of our church lives, we'd see the results that Jesus and the early church saw.

Desert Island Worshippers

So we stopped all music and began a journey, discovering what prayer, corporate worship and public gatherings may have been like for the early church. We actively redesigned our concept of worship from a spectatorship model into a participatory model.

We did this by saying we were aiming to become Desert Island Worshippers, posing the question: If you were on a desert island, and had no CD player, no worship leader or Bible reading plan, would you still worship, pray, hear God, follow the Spirit and meet with God easily? If not, why not? I wanted every individual worshipper in my church to be a Desert Island Worshipper, believing that God's presence would be far more powerful among us corporately if we were all engaging with God in prayer and worship and following the Spirit as individuals.

For three months it was hell! We taught and taught: how to meet God, how to come into the throne room, how to pray fervently, how to hear God's voice, sing in tongues, overcome the feelings of the flesh and be an initiator instead of a spectator in worship. (Some of these lessons make up part two of this book.) Congregation members begged me, on their knees, to play some music: 'Please – just one little note to help us feel like worshipping!' they said. My resolve complete, we struggled on through the pain barriers to reach a new place in worship – and it was worth it.

The Mountain Top

After three months of painful growth, we arrived at our first mountain top. We could now pray in the Spirit, crying out in intercessions for half an hour at a time on a Sunday morning. I remember seeing young children weeping, crying out to God for the lost. At times we had to shout out to guide the enthusiastic prayers, they were so fervent! I saw people saved right in the middle of our praying in tongues. I recall seeing a visiting leader's wife refuse to come into our building, kneeling in the entrance, saying, 'The holiness of God is too strong in there – I can't go in!' I remember the congregation, children included, singing in tongues for over an hour at a time without musical backing. I remember a service when God said, 'No meeting; just fellowship together,' so we did.

I remember meetings that were an hour long; I also remember a nine-hour service as God moved upon us. I remember seeing people healed as we sang. I recall people walking to the front in tears, overcome by God's presence – we had simply sung in tongues.

As far as we knew how, we let God lead our services. You never knew what would happen next: prayer, listening to God, team ministry, preaching, prophetic action, quietness, spontaneous song, teaching, dancing. Some meetings were all teaching, others all worship; others were family services or fun times. We made many mistakes, but that was covered in love and the fruit was worth it.

Revolutionised Prayer Lives

One amazing characteristic of this move of God was the effect on personal prayer lives. Within a few weeks congregation members began to tell me their prayer lives had been transformed, because they now did things in church that they could do at home. They knew how to pray, what to pray, how to hear God, follow the Spirit and overcome the apathetic feelings of the flesh that fight against true prayer and worship. Something that had been a mysterious discipline of the spiritually mature had now become the corporate and personal joy of every church member, children included. Surely this is the same mountain top that every revivalist has seen prior to a great move of God?

Bringing Back the Music

The amazing thing was that for months not a note of music was played. Many would not have thought it possible in our culture. Yet there we were, in the 1990s in Yorkshire, England, seeing a vibrant congregation of believers praying and following the Spirit as the early church had done! Even today when I return to visit that church there is an unusual sense of passionate worship. Something had happened that can never be lost in the lives of the individuals involved.

After several months, we restored music to our 'new' worship. It was like adding petrol to a fire! The music ministry had become what I believe God intended it to be: a tool to enhance and accompany the worship of a powerful, prophetic, self-initiating body of believers.

Do You Have the Courage?

Please do not take this to mean that I believe everyone should remove their musicians. That was simply our method for that time. I am not against music ministry in any way. Indeed I am a musician, singer and songwriter myself.

But I do believe we have so overemphasised programmes and music ministry that it has weakened the local church, making us entertainment-centred and self-ish. Music can be powerful but it can also be a crutch, creating high-maintenance Christians to whom revival would be alien, as revival is neither entertaining nor comfortable. I also believe we have underemphasised prayer, resulting in a prayer-shy western church. We can attempt to redress the balance through many prayer initiatives, but nothing will equal the establishment of fervent prayer in the centre of our church services.

I believe we have become programme-orientated. Tozer said: 'We replace presence with programme.' How true! Is our current blueprint for church welcoming to the presence of God? Have we built a temple for his presence, or for our music, plans and performances? I believe many of us should question our design honestly before God and discover whether we are hosting him or an inherited Christian culture. While our church culture may pay lip service to God and his presence, is it truly electrified by his Spirit's approval? Are we ritualistically honouring God in a design that was once relational and

Spirit-led, while God has moved on and is waiting to pour his glory into a new wineskin?

I believe many of us have become prayerless and powerless. We have become theatre houses, entertainment centres, intimidated by our modern society and its shallow post-modernism; a culture where immediate happiness is the god, 'microwave' spirituality is fashionable and no one has the right to challenge anyone else, as personal rights supersede any ultimate truth.

But I also believe we can go beyond that culture. We can re-establish the kingdom in people's thinking and become powerhouses of prayer and the presence of God once again. We can lead our people into the glory of God. We can follow the Spirit as great men of old have done. We can pray fervently in church on a Sunday, worship loudly and passionately, pray in the Spirit, walk in the unpredictable power of God and carry his presence so powerfully that unbelievers come running into our churches asking to be saved.

We can, if we have the courage to redesign our churches for the presence of God.

The Challenge of the Chapter

- Music can, at times, actually hinder true worship.
- Have songs replaced prayer at your church?
- Has ritual replaced relationship in your life, ministry or meetings?
- Has entertainment replaced cost, death to self and sacrifice?
- Has programme replaced God's presence in your meetings?
- Do you have the courage to prayerfully seek the culture of heaven, rather than following western Christian culture?

Chapter 4

THE EIGHT GREAT MYTHS OF WORSHIP

Is your Messiah made in your image?
Is your Jesus under control?
Is your religion made for your glory, or his?

Three signs discussed in the preceding chapters marked my initial journey in redesigning my own church worship for God's presence. In subsequent years I have realised there were many other misconceptions, myths and fallacies in my thinking that affected my worship ministry. Subtly they may infect all our thinking, dulling our understanding of God's plan for hosting his presence among us. Here are a few common myths that have led our worship into what it is today.

Myth No. 1: God's Order is Like Our Order

Church can either be a mortuary or a nursery. Now while a mortuary may be clean, disinfected, tidy and orderly, it is a place of death. Life is messy – you can't avoid that. A nursery is full of life: noise, mess up the walls, funny smells and big mistakes. But it's life, wonderful life! People learning, growing, feeding, sharing and laughing. People developing, discovering, relating and searching.

We should not be trying to develop an 'orderly' worship service where God's presence has no room to move and no mistakes can be made. We should not be trying to be too tidy and polished in our week-to-week corporate worship. While I believe in excellence, God's presence and the smell of life are far more precious. Be excellent, but be soft enough to let him overwhelm your excellent offerings with his power. That may be messy. Remember my dancing Mexican friends from the first chapter, who though excellent in worship were willing to be overwhelmed by God. That was one small outer sign of this church of six thousand that was experiencing a glorious revival.

Someone once said: 'The church should be the training place for the market place.' It should be a place of learning and growth, like a nursery. Now I know you're going to use that 'God is not a God of disorder' verse on me, but you must understand that God's order is not British or designed for your culture. God's idea of order may be the day of Pentecost, with people looking drunk and babbling in tongues. His order may be like the temple, so filled with glory that people are unable to do their work. God's order can be loud and fervent – zealous to the point of throwing salesmen out of the house of God! You've only got to read a few pages of Scripture to realise that at times God overwhelms earthly situations with heavenly 'order'. Does your blueprint for worship allow for the fact that God's culture and our culture may be quite different? If you are seeking to host God among you, you must design for his eternal culture, rather than our temporal culture. Once we are impacted by heaven, we soon see the shallowness of our own era's demands. True temples of glory are far more attractive to the world than any skilful imitation of its own pleasure centres.

Myth No. 2: God is Polite and Politically Correct

We live in a PC age. Everyone and everything has to be politically correct. But God might not be. Offence is a part of his Gospel. Remove its offence and you remove something of its power. It's not meant to fit in. It's not meant to soothe the world into heaven. The early church brought fear to cities, looked a little drunk at times, yet saw thousands saved. Jesus' language was pretty rich, his disciples pretty raw, and his Holy Spirit's outpouring pretty riotous!

On the day of Pentecost, Peter stood up and proclaimed that he knew who the Messiah was (that's the first reason why the thousands gathered could have killed him). In the next breath he's telling this growing crowd that they killed their Messiah – the Son of God they had been expecting for hundreds of years (there's a second reason for a good stoning). Amazingly, three thousand of those gathered were cut to the heart at his words and surrendered their lives to Christ.

We must stop trying to impress the world with our songs and well-ordered services. We must start to experience God's powerful presence among us. We must move in signs and wonders and see, as great revivalists like the Wesleys did, God move among us and shake the congregations and contents of our meetings. This will not be accomplished through polished music, polite messages and politically correct ministry. The kingdom comes through the violent, zealous actions of a church on fire for God.

Myth No. 3: The Local Church Should Be Like a Conference

One of the great yet subtle pressures on church leaders today comes from our church culture of camps and conferences. Once a year, many in our churches go on an exodus to wonderful camps where thousands congregate. The greatest preachers preach and the worship (especially the music) is often outstanding.

While I love conferences, the subtle error that such gatherings may teach us is that we need to recreate the conference at home, with amazing music and concert-style worship in our local church meetings. While that may be great for one-off events, special celebrations and camps, it should not be the bread and butter design of week-to-week church life. It breeds weak, entertainment-centred Christians, who are quite happy to sing their way to heaven yet rarely engage themselves in corporate prayer, body ministry, deep intercession and other necessary local church activities.

Myth No. 4: If in Doubt, Do What You Did Last Week

Many of us have a pattern of worship service. If God doesn't speak clearly to us, we normally slip straight back into that pattern. But I tend to think that if God doesn't tell me to do something, I can do whatever I want. I can use my imagination and make a meeting interesting and exciting. I don't have to fall back on what we already know. I can keep the congregation supple and expectant by being creative and interesting.

God has made us in his image, and that means being imaginative and creative. We are alive, which means we should develop, change and grow. This should be expressed in our worship, as we use all our God-given faculties to lead the people of God to his throne.

Myth No. 5: Better Music Will Mean Better Worship

I am regularly asked to speak to worship groups. The request usually comes from a church leader sincerely wanting to see an improvement in the area of worship in their church. On meeting worship groups I often reach the opinion that the issue of improving worship lies not with the music, but with the congregation.

In many cases, the way to improve our worship may not be by getting better at music or by increasing the spirituality of our worship teams. Better music will give us a better-looking meeting, but it may not actually improve the worship or the manifestation of God's presence. We quickly reach a ceiling in what we can accomplish in church by becoming more musically skilful. There comes a point when we have to thank the music group for all their hard work, face the congregation and let them know it is they who need to grow. That will only come by teaching, training and leading the congregation to a new place in God. The congregation must go on a journey of worship, prayer and finding the presence of God together, where they learn to facilitate the glory of God as a family of believers, rather than expecting musicians to miraculously usher heaven to earth each Sunday.

Myth No. 6: Our Worship Culture is the Right One

It is primarily the USA and Europe that spearhead the world's most high-profile trends in worship music today. It is these countries that have developed million-pound businesses in worship music, created pop-star worship leaders for us to admire (which in some way we should, of course), and churn out more worship resources than can possibly be bought. Many of these resources are outstanding and deserve our gratitude and time, but that does not mean that everything these nations are propagating is God's perfect prescription for corporate worship today. It simply means they have the money and technology to create renown and fame.

On a recent visit to Kenya, I ministered at a conference on worship where I taught many of the principles outlined in this book. As I taught, the congregation went bananas! They were jumping up and down and shouting – 'high fives' and loud Amens were aplenty!

After the conference, I asked my host why this sort of message might be so important to Africans. I presumed that they would be far more into power, prayer and the more costly side of worship than my own country, and that my message might be less relevant.

The Kenyan minister told me that there was great pressure from American and British worship ministries to develop the 'concert' style of worship in their churches. I reassured him that although America and Britain had good musicians and a high profile, it was African nations, South America and parts of Asia that were experiencing revival, and they'd be far better off using them as a model. The nations that propagate the current western worship scene are the very nations that are not in revival. You don't need to be a rocket scientist to work out the relevant connections.

I believe that as God moves on North America and Europe in the coming decades we will see a great change in our worship. Fervent prayer will become far more central. The worship will become far more exuberant, passionate and unpredictable. God will overwhelm meetings as our leaders learn to step aside and allow the Holy Spirit to lead our services, resulting in mighty out-pourings of the glory of God. I pray that we would become more like our neighbours in revival, not they like us, with our skilful yet presenceless programmes.

Myth No. 7: We Have to Fill the Allotted Time

One of the greatest hindrances to worship is that we feel we have to fill an allocated time slot. I don't know about you, but sometimes I feel that God has done all he wants to do in worship within fifteen minutes, but then we churn out a further forty-five minutes of song because 'it's the worship time' and someone somewhere has said it needs to last at least fifty minutes.

The problem with long, dutiful worship times, when God is obviously not present in a manifest way, is that many in the congregation become bored. This leads to a lack of expectancy and excitement, which in turn leads to worship times worsening as the weeks go on.

I think it is far better to have great, short worship times, where we only 'go on further' when God really turns up. This leads to greater excitement, and a sense that leaders won't keep going if it's not happening. After all, who said that worship has to last a certain length of time, or that it has to happen in every meeting at all?

Of course, at times the lack of a sense of God's pres-ence is due to a congregation's apathy or poor under-standing of worship, rather than the Spirit's leading to stop. In this case, when a worship time is not 'happening', I recommend we stop and teach, through example and instruction, what is required from the congregation to follow the Spirit for that meeting. A willingness to stop and teach or deal with problems, rather than wading through our song list, should mean we never have to endure a boring worship time.

On the other hand, how often do we end a worship time just when it seems God is turning up? Sometimes preachers feel they have to give what they have prepared, whatever the presence of God is doing. Some preachers preach 'across' the anointing, instead of flowing with the Spirit of God.

I was hugely impressed by the renowned evangelist Don Double, who when hosting a large event in England patiently allowed many other ministers to speak while he sat to one side. He was scheduled to speak on the final night, a task I'm sure he was itching to get on with.

The final night arrived and I was invited to sing before Don came to speak. As I sang and people worshipped, God's presence seemed to invade the auditorium. It was as though we were on the very brink of glory. Once my song was finished, I presumed Don would quieten things down and preach his message. To my delight and surprise he stood and simply invited us to go further into God. For the next hour we were engulfed in the wonder of worship, with many prostrate before the Lord, many healed and many touched by God. Don never did get to preach. We can all learn a lesson from that humble man.

Myth No. 8: Well, it Works in Pensacola!

Imitation floods the ranks of the church. Sadly, there are very few originals. There are very few who will seek

God and find his blueprint for a life, a church, a meeting or a ministry. We kick into autopilot week after week, churning out what we've seen in other churches, camps and conferences. We must learn that the most powerful place to be in God is to be an original. Imitations can be good, but they are still only good imitations. Every time you take one step away from the original, the power of God decreases. People imitate styles, even down to dress sense, running orders and album covers. While imitation is flattering to the imitated, it can also show a remarkable lack of authenticity, a value close to God's heart. He demands that we worship in truth, meaning reality or authenticity (John 4:23).

A friend of mine was ministering in Indonesia, where one church mimicked the complete running order of a well-known American worship album, right down to the ad-libs and the talking between the songs! The funny thing was that the American who recorded the album is a big black Gospel singer, so it looked hilarious for a little Indonesian man to be impersonating him!

How on earth can God's glory come to us when we are a mere facsimile of the real thing? God comes to real people in real situations offering real worship – no matter how feeble or skilful, polished or not. History shows us God comes to honest, authentic worship, whether that's a cry in a desert or a heartfelt wail of intercession. People who are imitating a well-known worship leader or style are simply comic catastrophes, more suited to a TV show where the public attempt to mimic their favourite pop idol. That's pantomime, not the church of the living God.

Imitation reveals that we have a lack of relationship with God; that we fail to dig wells for his wisdom in our lives. It is, after all, far 'cheaper' to imitate than to find God for yourself. It also shows that we are dissatisfied

with ourselves, and that we perhaps consider other giftings and people of more value to God. Now I know I am
far from the most talented singer or worship leader – but
I must appreciate what I have been given. I must learn to
run in that anointing and be myself, because I'm precious. I must overcome insecurities and jealousies and
be content to be myself, with all my flaws and failings.
God still has a plan for me. He still wants to use me – not
me being someone else. It is Christ in me that is the hope
of glory, not Christ in a pantomime!

I was ministering some years ago at a conference in
Scotland. At one point in the day a dozen or more people gathered at the front for healing. Starting at one end
of the line I laid hands on the sick and, looking and
sounding as authoritative as I possibly could, I commanded the sickness to go. Nothing happened.

After about four people, I finally admitted to God that
nothing was happening and I didn't know why. God
whispered to me: 'You're on autopilot. You're just doing
what you've seen others do when praying for the sick.
You haven't asked me what I want you to do.'

Apologetically, I started again from the end of the
line, and this time, instead of trying to look spiritual, I
simply did what God told me to do with each person.
With some it was a word. With another I was to blow on
them (this worried me as I'd had garlic!). Some I laid
hands on, for some I commanded demonic influences to
leave, while with others I simply stood nearby.

As I did just what God told me to do each time, the
power of God came and touched lives. One woman fell
to the ground. Later she told the story of her healing. As
she hit the floor she found herself moving down a tunnel to a bright light. She entered a garden at the end of
the tunnel, met Jesus, and he healed her of an incurable
disease! Many others were also healed.

The most powerful place in God is to be an original. You don't impress God or woo him to your temple by saying: 'This is what we saw so-and-so do and you turned up.' No, he wants to give you *his* blueprint, for *your* temple! A one-off, intimate expression written in God's handwriting on your heart.

The Challenge of the Chapter

- God's order is not like our order.
- Church should be like a nursery, not a mortuary.
- Do you think God could ever be offensive, angry or unusual?
- Have you fully trained your congregation to worship and pray?
- Worship does not need to go on a long time to be good worship.
- Imitation is unauthentic worship. Are you copying someone else?

Chapter 5

PREPARING A WAY FOR THE LORD

> *In the desert, prepare a way for the Lord*
> *Make straight in the wilderness a highway for*
>   *our God*
> *Every valley shall be raised up*
> *Every mountain and hill made low*
> *The rough ground become level*
> *And the rugged place a plain*
> *And the glory of the Lord shall be revealed.*

Perhaps you are now as thoroughly frustrated with worship as I have been. Perhaps many of the things I have shared in these first few chapters have rung true in your own heart. Perhaps, like many of those who attend my seminars, you would like to say: 'I've thought that for years. It's nice to hear someone say it!'

Now comes the hardest part: Once a word from God has touched our heart we are responsible for it. Faith without action is dead. The wise man was not the one who heard the word of God, but the one who acted on it.

So now, like me, you may be longing to lift your congregation to a higher place in worship. You may want to teach and train your people, redesigning your worship culture so that God's glory may dwell among you. You may think it is time that, like John the Baptist, you prepared a way for the Lord to come in glory. It's time to level the mountains and raise the valleys.

If you do, you will need some tools to help carry your people through this time of change. Levelling mountains for his coming takes skill and hard work. Surprisingly, we cannot simply turn to our people and say, 'Let's stop what we're doing and follow the Spirit.' We have become so used to our culture of song-singing and listening to sermons that taking our churches to a new place will require new skills on their part. I personally do not want to leave anyone behind when moving forward in God. I want to use every tool possible to gather people together and move us forward as a single unit in God.

As we led our church from concert-style worship to a Spirit-led model of corporate worship and prayer in the early 1990s, we learned that the following points helped to create an atmosphere of expectancy and journeying forward into a new level.

Teach, Teach, Teach

I was once at a media conference in London where we learned about communication. This came in very handy when trying to take my congregation to a new dimension in worship. I learned that communication can be illustrated in terms of an aeroplane. The plane taking off is an illustration of our speaking a certain truth. Once the plane has taken off and we have said what we want to say, we believe we have communicated.

However, communication is about more than just a plane taking off. It is also about when the plane lands. You have only communicated effectively when the plane lands in the minds and hearts of those you wish to communicate with. Sometimes the plane of your communication has to take off a dozen times before it will land in a person's heart.

I experienced this clearly over our period of redesigning worship as a church. During our most painful three months I had to teach and teach, with numerous 'planes' taking off again and again. Slowly but surely different people caught the vision of going higher and following the Spirit in worship. At first many didn't understand why we should change our worship culture at all, or why we should expect more than singing a few songs and listening to sermons. But week by week I saw the plane land in more lives. It was deeply satisfying as different ones would come up and say, 'Ah! Now I understand what you're getting at!'

In order to take your church higher you must teach and teach in a huge variety of ways. Some understand verbal communication, others prefer visual, others learn by experiencing, touching and feeling a truth. Many leaders teach one sermon on worship and expect their church worshippers to change overnight. We must teach and teach, over and over again, until people deeply catch where we want to go. It is the only way to change a whole culture and understanding in the minds of the people we are called to lead.

Develop Momentum

Momentum is a vital tool for developing your congregation. As you build up momentum, moving from lesson to lesson, you create an increasing expectancy.

Teaching once a year on worship will not radically affect the culture of worship in your church. You need to hit the area of worship for a consistent amount of time, rising higher and higher. Devote a whole series of teaching to worship, have several conferences over a few months and get your home groups learning the subject. Use every conceivable communication tool to lift your people to a new level. Invite individuals gifted in worship to minister, invest time and training in your worship team and make worship resources available to your congregation. Don't be afraid to use workshop-style teaching on a Sunday morning or to teach on worship or prayer during the worship time.

Redesign Your Leadership Structure

In some churches, leadership structures do not lend themselves to the moving of the Spirit in meetings. People are given slots to fill: worship leaders fill their slots with singing and teachers fill their slots with words. If you really want God to move in your church, you need to redesign your leadership structure to be supple enough for God to speak, for you to hear, and for the church to follow.

Can God stop the worship? If so, how? If the planned singing item is not going to happen, how is this communicated? Can the worship be interrupted with a ministry time? What happens if God wants to do something different in your church? How are prophecies brought from the body of believers to the church in a meeting?

My personal preference is to have meetings led by experienced ministers, people of the Spirit who will do their utmost to follow God when he wants us to pray, sing, dance, receive, listen, minister, intercede or praise.

The musicians should be on hand to support and provide music when it's needed, which may be a lot in a meeting or may be just a little. In some cases a musician may be mature and gifted enough to lead in more than just singing, in which case they may be able to lead a whole service themselves. Many musicians, however, are restricted in that they are only mature enough or gifted to lead songs, which will leave a multitude of Spirit instructions ignored and unheard during a service.

If we desire God's manifest presence among us, we must put in place a leadership design that allows for the unpredictable leading of the wind of the Spirit. In whatever way possible, use your musicians, leaders and worship leaders, taking into account all their various giftings, functions and limitations, to establish a meeting leadership team who can follow the Holy Spirit wherever he leads you.

Refocus Your Songs

One of the most powerful things I've noticed as a worship leader is that when we find truly worshipful songs, the atmosphere of a meeting can change. Now while many musicians may love a song for its groove or nice melody, I want worship to cause us to connect with God, not just with the music itself. There are certain songs that send the electricity of God crackling through a congregation. Many times I have been on the threshold of such glory only to find that a worship leader starts to sing an inappropriate song, chasing away the manifesting presence of God. Song choice is a great skill and requires spiritual discernment.

I like to see God worshipped in my services. There are many great teaching songs, many good prophetic songs and many great intercession songs, but it is in the God-focused worship songs that his presence is most tangible.

Worship, in my experience, is the most powerful place of God's glory. Now that may be in part because of my particular type of anointing in worship, but I would encourage you to look at the words of the songs you are singing, and what effect the words and musical style of a song have on your people. Does the song increase the sense of personal connection with God, or does it leave you simply singing 'about' God? Does it make people engage with God, or stand 'in the courts'?

It is amazing to see worship groups make the simple mistake of trying to get people worshipping to intercession songs, or trying to lead them into intimacy with God using teaching songs. Realise there is a difference and use the right songs for the right occasion. Don't be tempted to be too trendy in song choice. Just use that which connects people with the presence of God and that which causes the manifestation of his glory to fill your auditorium.

Better Musicianship

Finally, and without wishing to contradict anything I have said previously, improving your musicianship can sometimes have a good effect on your worship. In order to really follow the Holy Spirit in musical worship (remember, not all worship is musical), you often need to reach a certain level of skill. If, for instance, you want to be able to play without being glued to a list of songs or sheet music, you need to achieve a particular degree of musical ability. Also, although skill may not necessarily be connected to anointing, it is hard to facilitate the presence of God with a constant stream of badly played notes and out of tune singing!

On the other hand, you can be so skilful that God struggles to move through your music. Many classically trained musicians are so restricted by their training that there is little room for spontaneous musicianship. Worship expressed through music must be an expression of the heart, rather than a rendition of learned notes, if it is to be infused with the presence of God.

Climbing the Mountain

In conclusion, there are many, many skills that can dramatically ease our journey to a higher place in God. If you and your leaders are choosing to step up to a new place of worship and glory, then do so with careful thought, with great patience and with every skill and tool you can use in place.

I wish you every blessing in your journey as you seek to redesign your corporate worship for the glory and presence of God. May he fill, invade and utterly overwhelm your church, so that thousands will stream into the kingdom because of the light of his glory among you. 'For the Lord will rebuild Zion and appear in his glory' (Psalm 102:16).

The Challenge of the Chapter

- Do you want to change your worship culture to host God's presence more fully?
- Do you repeatedly teach on worship?
- You should develop momentum when teaching and training your church.

- Redesign your leadership structure, so the Holy Spirit can move unpredictably.
- Do your worship songs connect you with God?

PART 2

A BLUEPRINT FOR WORSHIPPERS

Your Majesty, I can but bow
I lay my all before you now
In royal robes I don't deserve
I live to serve your majesty.

Chapter 6

WORSHIPPING IN VAIN?

All I have, all I am, all I own
All I love, I lay down at your throne
I surrender.

True Worshippers, False Worshippers

'True worshippers will worship the Father in spirit and truth,
for they are the kind of worshippers the Father seeks' (Jn.
4:23).

God is looking for true worshippers. That implies that
there must be false worshippers. People who worship
the same God, the same Jesus, but their worship is false.
They are not the *kind* of worshippers the Father seeks.
Jesus himself makes it clear that to worship God is not
enough. There is a *kind* of worship he seeks. In the book
of Mark Jesus comes out with another startling statement: 'They worship me in vain' (Mark 7:7).

Now wouldn't you think that those who worship
Jesus are worshipping just fine? ('They worship *me*.') But
Jesus said: 'They worship me *in vain*.' In other words,
they were worshipping the right person but their

worship carried no value. It was pointless. Fruitless. Useless. Not appreciated by God.

I don't know about you, but I don't want to live life, pray, sing and applaud the Lord through all these meetings we have to attend, only to be told at the end of my life, 'All that activity was fruitless, pointless. You might as well not have done it.'

Worship is not a case of 'do what you feel like', as many churches openly state from their pulpits. No: worship includes certain important factors. There is a right and a wrong to worship. There is a worship the Father seeks and a worship the Father ignores. In the next few chapters of this book we'll look at some of the biblical priorities of praise and worship, to ensure that we don't worship God in vain but rather in such a way that he leaps from heaven into the situations of our lives with his manifest presence and power.

A Blueprint for True Worship

Just as corporate church worship needs a blueprint from heaven, so too the individual worshipper needs to fulfil a particular design. Many have taught that praise is powerful and that worship is exciting. We have all heard stories of visible glory and the power of God made manifest as believers worship. Praise seems to have caused cities to fall, prisoners to be freed and armies to be routed. But what kind of worshipper sees such results from his worship? What is true, powerful, heaven-moving worship?

What is Worship?

Some years ago a young worship leader asked God in prayer, 'Show me what true worship is.' Immediately he was taken in a vision behind the Iron Curtain and saw a man, imprisoned, being strapped to a table. Once his arms and legs were locked into place, several guards took batons and began beating the soles of the man's feet, breaking his bones, ripping open the skin and smashing away his toes.

The man's back arched and trembled with the pain as the guards screamed, 'Deny him, deny him!' The man opened his mouth, the guards still beating his feet into a bloody pulp, and wailed, 'I worship you, my Jesus! I will not deny you! I thank you for your love and for your cross. I will praise you while I have breath!'

God spoke into the heart of the young worship leader: 'That is worship.'

Another story is told of a prisoner of war assigned to stand in a pit of human excrement for years, cleaning and maintaining it. The prisoner, a godly man of true spirituality, stated at the end of his time there, 'I turned that place into a garden of worship.' So infused was he with the reality of his Saviour that, in the words of the old song, the things of the world grew 'strangely dim', and his inner light and life in Christ were unwavering.

These are men who understood true worship.

Cast your mind back to my dear friend Rita, from the introduction to this book, and allow me to recount one of her stories of the remarkable effect of a true, worshipping heart.

One day her local authorities invited Rita to speak to two warring tribes, to try to bring some semblance of peace. Taking her choir with her, she turned up and spoke to the roughest, toughest group of armed thugs you could ever dream of. She asked God, 'What shall I do, a little white woman among these violent men?'

On receiving instructions from God she proceeded to dance and praise, encircling the two tribes with her choir. On the seventh circumnavigation of the group, the glory of God fell, as did many of the tribal men gathered, leaving them sprawled on the dirt floor, where they wept, asking 'What is this?' She led many to the Lord that day, and introduced peace to the two villages.

These are the sorts of stories that leave us with the belief that praise and worship are powerful. But exactly what should the individual be doing in worship and what makes worship such a heavenly force? What are the basic raw ingredients that make the individual worship experience powerful, rather than just a singing of songs or the uttering of unanswered prayers?

The Challenge of the Chapter

- There is a right way to worship, and a wrong way.
- It is possible to worship Jesus in vain.
- True praise and worship are very powerful.

Chapter 7

YOUR MOUTH MOVES MOUNTAINS!

Sing to the Lord, declare his glory
Sing to the Lord, give him praise
In every nation proclaim his salvation
Say to the world 'Our God reigns!'

The first requirement if you are to be a powerful worshipper is to understand the very make-up of God himself, for we are made in his image. 'So God created man in his own image, in the image of God he created him' (Gen. 1:27).

We have been created in the image of God and there is one powerful characteristic of God that Scripture clearly states he has included in our make-up. It is a factor that plays a role in praise and worship and, under the leading of the Holy Spirit, can be a world-shaking force. It is the power of the tongue.

When reading the account of creation, it takes very little theological training to see that God made the earth and everything in it simply by speaking. Over and over again Genesis 1 states, 'And God said . . . and it was.' That was the power of God's words. A quick leap over to the end of the Bible and in Revelation we discover that God has not changed. Three awesome descriptions of Jesus give us a pictorial view of how this power works:

Out of his mouth came a sharp double-edged sword (Rev. 1:16).

I . . . will fight against them with the sword of my mouth (Rev. 2:16).

Out of his mouth comes a sharp sword with which to strike down the nations (Rev. 19:15).

In the mouth of Jesus we find a weapon, a force and a power. That's how he spoke and created the world. That's how he healed sick people with a word, commanded demons to leave and spoke to soldiers, making them fall over! It is because he has a power in his mouth.

The Power of Life and Death

'The tongue has the power of life and death, and those who love it will eat its fruit' (Prov. 18:21).

If we are made in the image of God, the words we speak will inherently contain power. The Bible clearly states that the tongue is a powerful source of life and death. With it we can bless and we can curse. Proverbs 11:11 states: 'Through the blessing of the upright a city is exalted.' That's amazing! A city's prosperity and happiness can depend on the words of blessing from the righteous. Proverbs also states:

The mouth of the righteous is a fountain of life (10:11).

With his mouth the godless destroys his neighbour (11:9).

The tongue of the wise brings healing (12:18).

That is attributing incredible power and influence to the words we speak. In the New Testament book of James, God goes a step further. He compares the tongue to the rudder of a ship. It's small, but it guides the whole ship of your life (Jas. 3:1–12). Everywhere you go, you go because of what you have said – your tongue providing direction for your life.

Don't Think About Problems, Speak to Them!

How often do we feel embarrassed about speaking things out? I have noticed that people who feel down don't often want to speak out. They want to 'think about the problem'. Ever been there? Of course the devil wants you to think about the problem. He wants you to analyse the mountain. To measure it. To compare it with other people's mountains. Anything but do what Jesus tells us to do with our mountainous problems: 'If anyone says to this mountain, "Go, throw yourself into the sea," and does not doubt in his heart . . . it will be done for him' (Mk. 11:23).

Don't think about the mountain. Speak to it! Move your tongue and release that atom bomb God has placed in your mouth! Swing that sword, fire that machine-gun, light that dynamite and level the mountain with faith in Jesus and the power he has given you.

Praise Should Be in Your Mouth

What has all this to do with praise and worship? Listen to this:

> *May the praise of God be in their mouths . . . to inflict vengeance on the nations (Ps. 149:6–7).*

Some people are obsessed about praise coming from the heart, so much so that they are afraid to let it out of their mouths. 'I'm worshipping in my heart, brother,' they say. Well, 'out of the overflow of the heart the mouth speaks!' God doesn't want praise to be simply in your heart. He wants the praise of God to be in your *mouth* as well. Notice that the result, according to this verse, is 'to inflict vengeance on the nations'. Psalm 149 goes on to say it will punish, bind and carry out God's sentence against the enemy. Praise in the mouth of a believer releases the arsenal of heaven into the atmosphere around you, binding the enemy and bringing the kingdom of God to your situation.

Paul and Silas were beaten up and in jail in Acts chapter 16. They did not feel like opening their mouths. They hadn't read the end of the chapter! They didn't know what God would do in response to their praises. But they sang out and adored God in the middle of their difficulties and God's presence invaded the jail, shaking away their chains and setting them free.

The power of God rides on the praises of his people. He somehow infects every faith-filled word with his authority, bringing all his kingdom's resources to bear in a situation. As we open our mouths in worship, the same glorious kingdom that is invading our hearts at God's throne invades the spiritual heavenlies around us. As we confess his lordship and pray under his inspiration with singing and rejoicing, all God's kingdom comes to earth. As we release our tongues to declare the wonders and lordship of Christ, the powers and principalities around us experience the same world-creating, devil-commanding, sickness-destroying power that God has in his own mouth. The very mouth that made the universe!

The first detail in the blueprint of a worshipper, then, is that you use your mouth to praise God. It is an overwhelmingly powerful ingredient, bringing heaven's power and authority into the very atmosphere where you live.

The Challenge of the Chapter

- God created the world by speaking.
- We are made in his image.
- Your mouth and words are a powerful force.
- Words make praise and worship very powerful.
- Don't think about problems, speak to them!
- Do you like to speak out your words of praise?

Chapter 8

PASSIONATE PRAISE

Clamorously foolish, humiliated in my eyes
A fool for God, undignified; someone that men
    despise
I'll sing like a bird, dance like a boy
Believe like a little child
Then I will be wise in the eyes of God.

Zeal is an overwhelming force. Psalm 22 states that God is enthroned on the praises of Israel. The word 'praise' here doesn't just mean singing a few nice songs, or thinking quietly about God. No, the word means 'high' praise. Praise that is fervent, loud, passionate. God is not enthroned in any old worship. He is enthroned in passionate worship.

That is why you go to some worship services and find that while they may be singing a few nice songs, God is not enthroned. There is no sense of his manifest presence. It's because people are not bringing the sacrifice of fervent praise. The flesh is still in charge. People are being entertained and are giving only a small amount of honour and respect to God.

But why are zeal, fervour and passionate praise so very important? To understand this we need to understand another aspect of the blueprint of God, a design aspect that links zeal with the advancement of the kingdom.

The Ever-Increasing Kingdom

Isaiah 9:7 says of Jesus: 'Of the increase of his government and peace there will be no end.' His government is his rule, his kingdom and his power on earth today. According to this verse it will never stop increasing. It is increasing as you read this book. There is more kingdom on the earth today than there was yesterday.

We want his kingdom and government to come into schools, colleges, universities, families, homes, workplaces, churches, friendships and a host of other situations. To do this we need his government to continually increase, because although he is in one sense 'Lord of all the earth', in another sense that lordship is still being experientially established day by day throughout every stratum of society and every nation of the earth.

Passion is God's Kingdom-Increasing Tool

So how does the government increase? How does the kingdom keep expanding into new lives and situations? The end of verse 7 tells us: 'The zeal of the Lord Almighty will accomplish this.' Zeal is God's kingdom-increasing tool.

Why do young Christians bring so many people to Christ? Is it because they're on fire for God and full of passion, or is it because they're so full of wisdom? Ha! It's because they are passionate and zealous! When some Christians become 'mature' they lose their zeal, and at the same time they lose their ability to truly advance the kingdom. They know more, but do less. Zeal, not knowledge, is the dynamic that increases the government of God. Ask anyone who has ever pioneered in anything and they will tell you that passion will take you places that knowledge alone never can. Now zeal must have knowledge added to it and that is good. But never lose your zeal. Knowledge without passion is just religion.

Passion in Praise and Prayer

Matthew 11:12 tells us that the kingdom of God is violently advancing. Violence, passion and zeal expand the kingdom. Not physical violence, of course, but excited and passionate people, who care deeply for the things of God and whose lives express that fervour.

The book of James tells us that it is the 'effectual fervent prayer of a righteous man' (Jas. 5:16, KJV) that sees results, not the sleepy, meditative petition. Sometimes we just want to get away with quietly thinking about God and offering a whisper of thanks to him. But while meditative worship has its place, the walls of Jericho fell to a shout, not a whisper!

Can you imagine if the Israelites had been British at the city of Jericho? We'd have loved the first few days of quiet walking. I suppose we'd have broken out the tea and cucumber sandwiches. When day seven arrived, though, I can imagine Joshua commanding us to 'shout, for the Lord has given you the city!' I can picture thousands of tweed-jacketed worshippers looking at Joshua from under their country caps and saying, 'Keep it down, old chap – this is church and we're British!'

I don't think the walls would have fallen down that day.

Fervour in worship releases us from our culture and the restraints of our fears. It pushes down the flesh and causes us to rely on the Spirit. It increases the kingdom as we worship, praise, evangelise and preach passionately about God and his ever-increasing kingdom and glory. So release the sacrifice of praise and advance the kingdom of God in your life through fervent praises. Your Jerichos will fall to passionate praises too.

The Challenge of the Chapter

- God's kingdom is always growing.
- Zeal and passion expand God's kingdom.
- Passion makes praise and worship very powerful.
- Do you pray with zeal and fervour as the book of James tells us to?

Chapter 9

THE CHOICE OF SPIRIT OVER FLESH

Overwhelmed by you
Overwhelmed by you
Purest of fires, changed my desires
In all you've done, I'm overcome
I'm overwhelmed by you.

'Yet a time is coming and has now come when the true worshippers will worship the Father in spirit and truth, for they are the kind of worshippers the Father seeks. God is spirit, and his worshippers must worship in spirit and in truth' (Jn. 4:23–24).

One of the primary characteristics of a true worshipper is worshipping in spirit. In fact, Jesus says we *must* worship him in spirit and in truth. There is no question about it – worship has to be 'in spirit'. Any other worship is false worship. Worshipping God in vain. So what does it mean to worship in spirit?

I am told that the book of John, where we find this statement by Christ, was written in such a way that we don't know whether Jesus was saying 'spirit' or 'Spirit'. As you will see, that makes little difference to us, and over the next three chapters we will look at three things we can learn from this scripture. They are that (1) we worship with our spirits, (2) we worship by the Holy Spirit and (3) we worship in the spiritual realm.

Let's examine the first of these statements.

Worship With Your Spirit

1 Thessalonians 5:23 states: 'May your whole spirit, soul and body be kept blameless'. This verse gives a convenient definition of our make-up as born-again people. We can clearly see that there are three parts to our being. We are spirits, who have souls and live in physical bodies. Worship is an activity that should find its source in our spirits, as opposed to our souls or bodies. Please understand that it will affect all of our being when we engage in worship, but the driving force must come from the spirit. To understand what that means, we must understand the difference between the three parts of our make-up and how they interact with each other and affect our lives.

Body, Soul and Spirit

Firstly, you live in a body. This is the physical 'tent' in which you live as a person. God has saved you and promises to 'give life to your mortal body' (Rom. 8:11). But you will one day lose your body through death and be given a new resurrection body at the coming of Christ.

Secondly, you have a soul. This is generally understood as your emotions, mind, desires and will. This is the part of you that is being constantly matured and developed into the image of Christ. When your soul acts independently of your spirit, this is what the Bible calls living in the flesh, or living by the sinful nature.

Thirdly, you are a spirit. Your spirit was dead (or separated from God) before you were born again. At the point of salvation God made your spirit alive, as his Spirit birthed new life within you. It's as though your spirit is re-energised towards God and comes alive towards him and in him. You are, from that point on, spiritually alive to God. In fact, God says you are now 'one with him in spirit' (1 Cor. 6:17).

Differing Desires

'For the sinful nature desires what is contrary to the Spirit, and the Spirit what is contrary to the sinful nature' (Gal. 5:17).

Here is a vital lesson to learn in the light of worship: because you are a three-part person, you have different drives and desire-sources stirring within you as a Christian. You have the desires of your body (e.g. I'm tired, hungry), the desires of your soul (e.g. feelings, logic, wants) and the desires of your spirit (e.g. conviction, obeying God's prompting, fulfilling truth).

Your spirit is the source of godly driving force. It is the avenue through which communication comes from God to you. Jesus said that the Spirit would guide us into all truth. This means that the Holy Spirit will constantly be igniting, inspiring and convincing you to fulfil God's desires, as God is truth.

Your soul and spirit each have desires that are asking for fulfilment. Often these different sources are crying out with opposite desires. A part of you will want to follow God, another part will be crying out to rebel. Like baby birds in a nest, straining open-mouthed to be satis-fied, each part of you calls out for attention. The impor-tant factor is to learn how to follow God and his will communicated to you through your spirit, whilst appre-ciating the very human needs of your soul and body.

In all of life, then, we have a choice. To live by the Spirit, or to live by our 'flesh'. In the context of worship Jesus makes it clear: true worshippers *must* worship in *spirit*.

David Told His Soul What to Do

David understood this when he sang, 'Praise the Lord, O my soul' in Psalm 103. He realised his soul would not always lead him as he should be led and might even rebel against his own spirit. He had to tell his soul to praise God. He also stated: 'Why are you downcast, O my soul? . . . Put your hope in God' (Ps. 42:5). He was saying 'C'mon soul, stop being miserable. Worship God!' He had the revelation that at times he had to deal aggressively with his sinful nature in order to live a godly life and follow God's Spirit.

Let's translate this to the area of your own worship life. When you get up early in the morning or attend a meeting at your church, your body may be crying out: 'I'm tired.' Your soul may saying: 'I'm fed up. I don't feel like God loves me.' But what truth is God's Spirit stir-ring in your spirit? 'Worship me, adore me, follow me; I love you, yield to me, I want to bless you.' He will be calling out to relate to you, asking for your surrender and worship. What do you do? Jesus said: 'True wor-shippers worship in spirit.'

The Challenge of the Chapter

- Worshippers must worship in spirit.
- You have a spirit, soul and body.
- You must worship led by your spirit, not by your soul or body.
- Your soul and body will often argue with your spirit, trying to stop you worshipping.
- Do you command your soul to worship when you don't feel like worshipping?

Chapter 10

GOD'S RIVER OF WORSHIP

Would you come and rest your glory on my life?
Would you come and overwhelm my world with
*   mercy and with might?*
Would you come and rest your presence in this place?
Would you cover me in glory?
Would you cover me in grace?
Would you cover me in power and send me from
*   this place?*

'It is we . . . who worship by the Spirit of God, who glory in Christ
Jesus, and who put no confidence in the flesh' (Phil. 3:3).

This leads us on to the next interpretation of that vital
verse in John 4 that tells us we should 'worship in
spirit'. As we have just learnt, we worship led by our
spirits rather than by our flesh, but in order to do that
there is something else we must do.

Worship *By* the Holy Spirit

When Jesus left the earth after his resurrection, he said to
his disciples, 'In a few days you will be baptised with the

Holy Spirit.' That word 'baptised' means to be immersed or dunked. He was saying he would sink us, immerse us and drench us in his own Spirit and presence.

Your spirit and God's Spirit must come into a state of glorious union if you are to be led by the Spirit in powerful worship. As you become one spirit with God through surrender and infilling (1 Cor. 6:17), his motives can become yours, his love becomes expressed in you and your worship is led and perfected by his own Spirit's leading. It is the Holy Spirit who will communicate to your spirit, giving direction, power, life and strength to your worship.

If we are to worship by the Spirit, we must worship as people drenched and covered by that beautiful gift, the Holy Spirit. Dry, fleshly worship is not enough. God wants wet, spiritual worship! Worship that will 'glory in Christ Jesus': inspired adoration, under the influence and leadership of God himself. God-centred, God-instigated, God-directed worship.

Rivers of Spiritual Worship

In John 7:37 Jesus invites us to drink from him if we are thirsty. He also tells us that after this, 'streams of living water will flow from within you'. This is a powerful picture, but what does it mean? We know he was talking about the Holy Spirit (he tells us that), but how will he 'flow from within us'? Will it be like some kind of blue liquid, bursting out of our belly buttons and streaming onto pavements, down streets and into houses, touching the world? No, of course not. I'm being silly to make us think about what we read!

When we drink of the Spirit, what are the streams that flow out from our innermost beings? I believe

Revelation 19:6 and the book of Acts give us a clue. Revelation says this:

> *Then I heard what sounded like a great multitude, like the roar of rushing waters . . . shouting: 'Hallelujah! For our Lord God Almighty reigns.'*

Could it be that the river that flows from within us when we drink of the Spirit is indeed a river of praise and worship? I believe it is.

It is amazing to see that every time the Holy Spirit is poured out in the book of Acts, there is a river of the voice of the church that flows in immediate response. Catch this and you will learn an amazing truth about worship.

When the Spirit is poured out in Acts 2, there follow streams of tongues declaring the wonders of God from the disciples. There is also a river of Gospel-preaching leading to three thousand salvations. (One mathematical Catholic priest reminded me that that was six born again for every word Peter used. That's the kind of fruit I want!) As you continue through the book of Acts you see that every drenching of the Spirit is accompanied by praise, prophecy, tongues or bold Gospel proclamation, all expressions of our worship. Think of it: every time we drink of the Spirit, a river of praise will flow out of us.

It is the Spirit at work within the church who releases rivers of praise, streams of worship and oceans of prophecy. It is the Spirit who releases riptides of bold preaching on streets and in workplaces and meetings. We don't want merely our clever songs or leadership styles, but the mighty river of the glory of God, pulsating throughout the church, making us fruitful witnesses and powerful praisers.

Let the Stream Flow

Learning the difference between our flesh and the promptings of God's Holy Spirit, in communion with our spirits, is a key to worship. Softening our hearts to yield to God and be filled to overflowing with his Spirit, and then letting 'the river' out of our mouths is essential. Developing an obedience to God's Spirit brings us into a realm that is far above the highs and lows of emotional experience. Above the realities of pews and song-singing. Far higher than the bored chanting of the prayer-hymn sandwich. It is the place where we lose our agendas and submit to his. We forget the songs and start connecting with God.

When we drink and let the streams flow from within us, we will find ourselves communing with God himself. Connecting to the life-flow of the Spirit of God, rather than singing 'at' or 'to' God. He will fill us, woo us, lift us and cause rivers of living water – indeed living worship – to pour out of our hearts in God-perfected praise. Praise that God has perfected himself is guaranteed to be accepted by the Perfecter: he knows what he likes! So drink. Drink deep. Get your congregation drinking deep, and let the streams of God burst into your neighbour-hood with praise and preaching.

The Challenge of the Chapter

- Worship should be led and empowered by the Holy Spirit.
- A river of worship will flow from you as you are filled with the Holy Spirit.
- Have you been baptised with the Holy Spirit?
- Are you seeking to be always filled with God's Spirit?

Chapter 11

THE INTIMACY OF GOD'S THRONE ROOM

Earth and heaven, worship you
Love eternal, faithful and true
Who bought the nations, ransomed souls
Brought this sinner near to your throne
All within me cries out in praise.

We have seen through the second section of this book that a worshipper must be passionate about God. We have learnt that the tongue of a worshipper moves mountains. We have understood that a true worshipper will rise above the lethargic influences of the flesh, to worship by the leading and infilling of the Spirit of God. All of these are thoroughly scriptural principles and may result in great power in and through our worship. Yet were we to end this section entitled 'A blueprint for worshippers' now, I feel we would still miss the very essence of worship.

What I have outlined so far could be considered as the scriptural scaffolding of a worship life. But there is a heartbeat that must be found. A core commitment of intimacy with God. A sense of deep and holy surrender to the Father. Without this, it could all be just 'a clanging gong' in the ears of God, and perhaps those around us. We have all met those 'worshippers' whose fervent dances are performed more for our eyes than for God's. Those babblers in tongues who would much rather 'pray' than obey. The cowardly 'worshippers' who seek permanent languid refuge from the real world and its needs in endless so-called worship. To engage in the form, while never finding the essence, is just empty religion.

Spiritual Worship and Spiritual Warfare

Most of the points made so far in this section of the book about the blueprint of a worshipper are to do with how the worshipper can impact the heavens and the spiritual environment in worship. It is about worship that seems to pray, intercede, and infect the atmosphere with God's presence, bringing about events like those seen in biblical times. Some would call it spiritual warfare.

You see, to me, worship is often prayer, and prayer is often worship. To praise, using words of life and passion that expand the kingdom, is an act of war against the dark forces of the enemy.

But now I want to speak not of the loud cries and passion that sparkle like electricity through the skies as we worship, 'binding' the enemy as Psalm 149 shows us; rather I want to speak of the heart of worship. The intimacy of our union with God. The throne room of God, where worship is more about relationship and less about warfare.

In opening this section of the book, I spoke of two prisoners who both held a deep devotion to God and his purposes, so much so that they were found worshipping in the direst of human circumstances. Their cry of worship rose above cruelty and pain, loneliness and death itself. I also spoke of my friend Rita, who brought God's glory into the African bush in the face of violence and aggression. These acts of worship come from a heart based not on formula or noise but on devotion to an intimate knowledge of God. These are men and women who have 'travelled' in worship to the feet of God. People who have been held in God's arms, have sought his face and heard him whisper in their ears. These are men and women who have been to the throne of God in the spiritual realm and can never be the same again.

The Throne of God

In the book of Revelation, we find a third and final application for the scripture we are studying, which states we should 'worship in spirit':

> *I was in the Spirit, and there before me was a throne in heaven with someone sitting on it (Rev. 4:2).*

Just like John in Revelation, I believe that when we worship in spirit we come before the very throne of God in heaven. Much of Scripture backs up this mind-blowing concept:

> *Let us then approach the throne of grace with confidence (Heb. 4:16).*

> *Since we have confidence to enter the Most Holy Place . . . let us draw near to God (Heb. 10:19–22).*

Do you realise what the Most Holy Place is? It is the very throne room of God. Jesus once entered God's throne room in order to make a way for New Covenant believers like you and me (Hebrews 9:24). When he died, the veil guarding his throne room was torn in two (Mt. 27:51) and Jesus made the way open for us to commune with God in all his holiness and utter intensity. Heaven was open. The throne room was accessible.

Approachable!

When Isaiah saw the Lord in all his glory in the sixth chapter of his book, the seraphs cried to one another, 'Holy, holy, holy'. The word 'holy' here means 'unapproachable'. The seraphs were warning Isaiah: 'Don't come near! Stay away! God is too pure and awesome for you.'

But Isaiah lived under the Old Covenant, where only the high priest could approach God's throne. Today, with the sacrifice of Jesus that took the punishment for our sins, the writer to the Hebrews boldly declares: 'Enter the Most Holy Place by the blood of Jesus, by a new and living way opened for us through the curtain' (Heb. 10:19–21).

In effect, God now cries out from heaven: 'Approachable, approachable! Come near – as near as you can.' He wants you to run into the intensity of his presence, knowing the wonder of the shed blood that has assured you a seat in the courtroom of the universe, the true tabernacle of heaven, the throne room of God.

Rather like the prophet who prayed for his servant's spiritual eyes to be opened so he could see into the spiritual realm, my prayer is that you would see this reality: as you worship in church gatherings, know that though your physical eyes may see seats, books, people and musical instruments, in spirit and reality you actually stand before the throne of God. As you worship in your car, at home, at work or in school, you are welcome in the arms of the Father, at the mercy seat where his glory dwells. His presence is no more present anywhere else in the world, or indeed the universe, than with you as you worship. Approach him, then, with confidence and discover the true essence of all worship.

Quieten Your Soul

I have spoken much in previous chapters of noise, dancing, sacrifice and fervour, as I believe these are often missing ingredients in western worship. But it should also be said that true worship must involve much reflection, wonder and quietness of soul in order for us to find the wells of worship bubbling up from deep within.

I have spoken of rivers of worship, but before any river can burst from our bellies, there is always the quietness of drinking from God's Holy Spirit. This is something quite different to the exuberance of spiritual warfare and praise, and if we are to be balanced and mature, we must understand that our worship will have both noise and quietness.

Some noisy worshippers (me included) love to quote the Jericho story when supporting their thesis for shouting – and I'm all for that. But we mustn't forget that six days of complete silence preceded the single shout. Quietness and contemplation in obedience to God are vital to prepare our souls for the battlefield of prayer and praise.

So come boldly to the throne. Kneel quietly, perhaps with no more than a groan or whisper of awe. Spend seventy per cent of your worship time listening to God's voice and waiting for the rivers of praise to bubble up from within you. Make sure that what flows from within you is a genuine stream of adoration, and not just the empty banging of words that come from no deeper than your voice box and rise no higher than the ceiling.

The Challenge of the Chapter

- The outward signs of worship are not enough on their own.
- Worship must go deeper than the 'acts' of spiritual warfare and prayer.
- You have access to the throne of God.
- Do you have an intimate relationship of awe and friendship with God?
- Spend much time listening to the voice of God.

Chapter 12

THE EIGHT ENEMIES OF A WORSHIPPER

They beat our faces and they whip our backs
Lock us in chains, put our feet in stocks
We praise his name
Praises don't know pain.

Worship and praise, prayer and spiritual warfare are all interconnected. In my opinion, to split them apart is to become too scientific in your approach. Somehow, as we follow God individually and corporately, listening to God, being filled with the Holy Spirit, praying, reflecting, singing or bowing – somehow in all the glory of that wondrous communion and communication, war is fought, the kingdom increases, our relationship with God is deepened and the atmosphere around us is changed.

But if praise, prayer and worship are so powerful, you can be assured that the devil will be doing all he can to hinder the worship of believers, both corporately and in personal prayer lives. In this chapter I want to outline eight major enemies of individual and corporate worship that the devil (and indeed our own culture or upbringing) will throw at us, dulling and undermining our worship lives.

Enemy No. 1: Fear

Fear is the enemy's chief weapon against most Christians, in most circumstances. It is the main cause of sin in most lives and it steals from the fullness of millions of people's lives and thousands of Christian meetings each year.

The reason why fear is so powerful is that it paralyses. It halts you in your tracks. The spirit of fear leads more church services than the Spirit of God does. It controls worship times, imprisons the gifts of the Spirit in us and turns the shout of victory into a whimper of embarrassment. It turns dancing into shuffling and creativity into predictable liturgy. It keeps us 'safe' from experimentation and guarantees the bland will always win. Fear is the sworn enemy of the river of true worship.

The apostle Paul addresses his young protégé in 2 Timothy 1:6, commanding him to 'fan into flame the gift of God, which is in you'. Paul is showing Timothy that there is something in him that is supposed to be a great big burning bonfire and it is his own duty to keep it blazing brightly. He must fan it into flame himself.

This tells us that Timothy's bonfire could easily become a smouldering ash heap if he wasn't careful. The supernatural energy and gifting from God could easily wane and dampen. And it is the same for you and me. There is a divine deposit of gifting and 'fuel' inside us that is so powerful, and yet so delicate, and it is our duty to keep it blazing. It is vital that we know what extinguishes the flame of the supernatural. In the next verse Paul goes on to show us the very thing that turns the blazing bonfire into a smouldering wick: 'For God did not give us a spirit of timidity, but a spirit of power, of love and of self-discipline.'

Fear is the fire extinguisher of all God's gifting within us. Do not allow it to take your praises and lock them in some predictable prison cell. Don't let fear lead your worship, don't let it dictate how loudly you can shout, whether you should kneel or not, or whether you can step out in the gifts of the Spirit. Ignore the feelings of fear and simply start doing the very thing that terrifies you. Fear will eventually stop knocking on your door.

Enemy No. 2: Religion

The second enemy of worship is religion. Not the kind of religion that speaks of caring for orphans and widows, intimacy with God and enjoying a healthy respect for our history and roots. But the kind that speaks of tradition, imitation, programmes, pride and worshipping the past.

A wonderful pastor was opening a new church and asked me to come and lead worship at the opening, a task I accepted. He told me that since they were a new church, they did not have a band, and so he had invited a band to play along with me. I was perfectly okay with this, until it slipped out that the band were not Christians!

Immediately my religious 'gland' set to work and a kind of righteous, all-knowing attitude seemed to cloud my every thought. 'How could these non-Christians follow the Spirit and move in anointed worship? They surely shouldn't play alongside me in the presence of a holy God!'

I asked the pastor to cancel the band, an assignment that he immediately accepted, then forgot.

The day came and in walked a group of highly colour-ful individuals, complete with Rasta hats, who announced to me, 'We are de band.' The 'distinctive' group had no doubt been gigging the night before, were a little hung over and smelt of an interesting mix of alco-hol, tobacco, and the Lord knows what else.

We began to practise and the band, who were all great musicians, immediately turned everything I played into Reggae. The meeting came and my well-polished wor-ship time turned into a Reggae party!

To my surprise, as the worship went on, we soon found ourselves singing in tongues and getting lost in rapturous worship! Within a few minutes it seemed as if God's presence rolled into the hall around us, people fell to the ground, and some screamed out, in need of deliv-erance.

Part way through the increasing 'mess' of heaven's touch, I noticed the guitar had stopped playing, and as the guitarist was behind me, I peered around to see why. There, just behind me, this wonderful young gui-tarist was kneeling, tears streaming down his face, giv-ing his life to Jesus. By the end of the meeting, his wife and child, who had come to watch, had also been saved.

It is amazing how my religiosity, my sense of right and wrong, sacred and secular, was completely different to God's. My upbringing, my arrogant sense of knowing 'how to do things' was actually nothing more than shal-low human religion, based on past experiences.

That day I heard a chuckle from heaven, as if God looked at me and said; 'Hey, little man, I'm the boss. You just do what I tell you to do. I'm actually not that both-ered about your opinions!'

Enemy No. 3: Guilt

The third great enemy of worship is guilt. It amazes me how Christians, who are supposed to be the forgiven ones, the righteous ones and the loved ones, actually seem the most miserable at times. It is as if all of Christianity so often forgets the central fact that God forgives our sins.

Religious Christianity can so quickly become a guilt trip, as some preaching only seems to heighten the sense in many of us that we never quite do things right. We never pray enough, love enough, sing enough or attend enough. The Christian life becomes full of things we feel duty bound to do. This is a million miles from the Gospel Jesus taught.

Always remember the wondrous love of God, the greatness of his grace and the riches of his mercy. He loves you completely. He doesn't give us a licence to sin, but he does want us simply to confess our sins, receive forgiveness and walk as best we can in his will. As we come close to him, it is he who will help us to live lives worthy of the calling he has given us. Don't allow guilt to keep you from God's presence. Confess your sins and receive forgiveness by faith.

Enemy No. 4: Agendas

Another great enemy of worship is to be always looking for an agenda in it. People often struggle to get 'lost' in worship. They are waiting for the next song, or the next item in the meeting. Actually, God often just wants us to hang out with him.

One of the greatest things to do is to learn to 'be' in God's presence. To relax, lose all programmes and just 'be'

with God. Loving him, worshipping, sometimes not saying or praying anything. Just basking in his Holy Spirit.

I wrote a song many years ago that included these
words:

> *Deep calls to deep in the roar of your waterfalls,*
> *All of your breakers have swept over me.*
> *The longer I dwell near the whispers of your heartbeat*
> *The more of your nature I'm finding in me.*

And that's the truth. When we pray, worship and rest in
God's presence, though it may seem little is happening
(i.e. there may not be a great agenda or prayer requests,
visions from heaven or a good song list) the truth is that
God does something deep within our spirits. We may
only see the change in ourselves when we leave the time
of worship and prayer.

I believe that as we worship, waves of God's nature
crash like the sea, deep upon the shores of our spirits,
and cause his goodness to flood us, making us more
fruitful and more intimate with him.

When you come to worship, whether alone or with
many, stop waiting for the leader to lead you. Stop thinking
you need a grand agenda. Just hang out with God. Lovers
don't need plans and programmes to enjoy themselves.
They just spend time loving each other, holding hands,
looking into each other's eyes and whispering sweet noth-
ings to each other. If we become lovers of God in this way I
believe we'll see more of his nature in our lives.

Enemy No. 5: Unforgiveness

When the Spirit of God descended at Pentecost, the book
of Acts chapter 2 shows us that the disciples 'were all

with one accord in one place' (KJV). This actually means they were of one mind and purpose. Also, when the singers and musicians joined 'as one' at the temple's dedication in 2 Chronicles 5, the cloud of God's glory filled the temple so powerfully that no one could stand. From these scriptural events we find another lesson for us about worship, and it concerns unity and unforgiveness.

Unity is a vital ingredient in the habitation of God's Spirit in a corporate worship meeting, family home or team situation. Jesus made it quite clear that if we have something against our brother or sister, we should deal with that first before bringing our offerings to God. Clean and loving relationships, gathered around united purposes, are important if we desire the manifestation of God's glory in our churches and homes.

I recently heard a wonderful Anglican bishop teaching on worship, who spoke of a truth that revolutionised my thinking about worship. He said that we never really worship alone, that there is no such thing as 'personal worship'. Why? Because we always join with the glorious church of God when we worship, and that church knows no geographical boundaries, as she always worships in the spirit and not in the restrictions of geography or flesh.

Whenever we worship, even if we are alone in our home, we are actually joining with millions of worshippers around the world, and countless angelic beings in the heavenly places gathered around the wondrous throne of God, to offer praise, thanks and our whole lives to him in adoration.

So as you worship, remember you are part of a whole. When we come in worship, in a sense we lose our individuality, joining with the family of God in heaven and on earth to worship at his footstool. Make sure, as you approach his throne, that you love and support the family you worship alongside, or you may grieve the heart of God.

Enemy No. 6: Seeking Experiences

The sixth area of concern for those of us who want to enjoy a full and fruitful worship life is hunting for endless spiritual experiences.

In reading this book you may have been inspired, possibly even impressed, by some of the stories of worshippers enjoying manifestations of God's presence in visions, dreams and healings or in signs and wonders. While the heart of this book is to see more of the Holy Spirit's movement in our churches and lives, there may also be a danger that we think that if we do not experience visions or spiritual feelings on a daily basis, there may be something wrong with us. This is simply not true.

When we read some books of the Bible, we may at times be tempted to assume that prophets are having daily visions, that every encounter Jesus had was miraculous and that God is interested in handing out mystical experiences on a daily basis. Nothing could be further from the truth, and to live our lives based solely on how we are feeling or what we are experiencing is a mistake.

Many of the prophets had many, many years between recorded visions. Jesus had thirty years during which we have next to nothing of interest to say in the area of the miraculous. God the Father is far more interested in dealing with issues of character, maturity and servanthood than he is in giving us visions and experiences. Because of this he may not grant us overwhelming experiences for long seasons in our lives.

But worship should not halt in those seasons when 'nothing is happening'. It is vital that we worship with discipline and regularity, even when we don't feel like it. I go through times of hearing God's voice loudly and clearly. Times when it seems obvious to me what his will is. Times when I feel his love and times when I am drunk on his presence, as in Acts chapter 2. But I also worship through long seasons when I'm simply chatting with God, trusting, learning character development and hard lessons. Some call them 'dry times' or 'wilderness years'. I simply call them the ebb and flow of natural life.

In all areas of life there are exciting times and boring times. Growing times and pruning times. Times full of good feelings and times full of dry decisions. Times when you feel in love, and times when you just love because of commitment. That's life. Worship through it all, still knowing by faith (not sight or feelings) that you worship before God's glorious throne. Worship in truth whether you feel like it or not.

Enemy No. 7: Hypocrisy

One of my great fathers in the faith, who recently went to his reward in heaven, was John McKay. I remember how when I was at Bible school this wonderful Scottish scholar, so remarkably filled with the Spirit, said, 'Christians don't tell lies; they sing them in their songs.' This memorable line speaks of another enemy of true worship.

Many people make the noise of worship, while their lives do not match their words. We sing of surrendering to Jesus, of loving others, of bowing our lives before God – and yet we live selfish, arrogant, rebellious, unforgiving lives. This cannot be!

I heard one leader speak recently of a conference at which he was preaching, where hundreds of young people gathered to worship, pray, cry out and dance before God each night. One evening he preached and there was a wonderful time of ministry, kneeling, bowing and surrendering to God. That night, though, many of those gathered went back to their tents to have sex with their girlfriends and boyfriends! The next morning they gathered to 'worship' once more as if nothing had happened. This is tempting the judgement of God and many, like Ananias and Sapphira (Acts 5), may eventually know the punishment of God if they do not humble themselves. Please God, have mercy on us.

Enemy No. 8: Pride

'Therefore I urge you, brothers, in view of God's mercy, to offer your bodies as living sacrifices, holy and pleasing to God – this is your spiritual act of worship. Do not conform any longer to the pattern of this world . . .' (Rom. 12:1–2).

These great words from the letter to the Romans touch upon what I believe is the eighth enemy of worship. There is something about worship that is sacrificial in the area of our pride, as it demands that we use our bodies.

In the west there seems to be a separation in the mindset of believers between our hearts and our bodies, as if we can worship with our hearts without engaging our mouths or bodies. Some would even suggest that our hearts offer spiritual worship, while our bodily praises could be considered fleshly and less vital. Now while I understand that what most are trying to do is avoid hypocrisy and shallowness, these verses actually refute the theory that bodily worship is any less spiritual than that of the heart.

The apostle Paul states here that offering your body to God in worship is a *spiritual* act of worship, not merely physical. The point is that there is something about using your body that is an important part of making your worship 'in spirit and truth'.

To me, the reason for this is that using your body in worship hits at the very heart of pride, and surrendering our pride in worship is perhaps the deepest, most costly adoration we can offer. I am amazed by the number of women who shout at their kids but who struggle to offer a shout of praise to God. I am dumbfounded to hear of men who dance in a nightclub but who stand like stone statues in corporate worship. I am flummoxed to see people who can put washing on a washing line yet struggle to raise their hands in worship!

There is something about physical worship that hits deep at the core of our pride, and so pride becomes an enemy of true spiritual worship. Our physical worship becomes the truest reflection of our heart's state.

In 2 Samuel 6 we find the well-known story of David dancing like a madman, bringing the Ark of the Covenant into Jerusalem. His wife Michal despised him for this, and bore no children afterwards. How many Michals are there in your church that despise the 'crazy' worshippers who just want to give God everything, pride and reputation included? Sadly there are many. And perhaps they too will struggle to bear fruit, as their pride closes up their worship life and intimacy with God. Perhaps you are a Michal yourself? I was.

I remember when God first told me he wanted me to have a worship ministry. I was as stiff as a surfboard in worship. My idea of dancing was to wiggle my fingers in my pocket! I was embarrassed at moving and bored by songs. But over a period of six months God slowly and tenderly set me free from my culture and myself, and I think that in many ways he is still doing that today. Why not join me in the adventure of becoming a true worshipper, the kind the Father is seeking?

Pride, programmes, experience-seeking, unforgiveness, fear, guilt, religion and hypocrisy: all enemies of the true worshipper. Why not come before God right now and pray through all these areas and see if there are any of these in your own life? Why not worship right now, wherever you are, and ask God to help you to become a temple fit for his glory?

The Challenge of the Chapter

- Does fear control your expression of worship?
- Are you religiously repeating the past, or looking for God's fresh blueprint for your worship?
- Is guilt keeping you from coming close to God?
- Try to worship without a set agenda – just enjoy God.
- Have you forgiven everyone who may have offended you?
- Does your lifestyle match your words of worship?
- Have you dealt with your pride and are you free to use your body to worship?

PART 3

A BLUEPRINT FOR LEADERS OF WORSHIP

Visions of glory fill my mind
Burned by your fire, sanctified
Ready to answer 'Here am I!'
I'm lost in your glory.

Lost in your glory, pilgrim at rest
Finally ready to touch this world I've left,
    with your glory.

Chapter 13

HANDLING THE PRESENCE OF GOD

> *The bloodstained way*
> *I've come the bloodstained way*
> *The doorway to your presence*
> *The pathway to your throne.*
>
> *For you are holy, holy, Lord God Almighty*
> *But I am holy only if I come the bloodstained way.*

To be in God's presence is wonderful. It is the atmosphere of heaven, the very reality of God among us. I don't want to merely sing about him, or to reverence him with my songs. I want to know him experientially. To sense him with me and in me and around me.

Of course, God is a holy God and his presence is a sensitive presence. We have all known his presence come and go. I have known him walk through a door right beside me; I have also known him leave a service when actions or attitudes offend him.

As a worship leader, you need to know how to care for the presence of God. You need to know what makes him stay and what makes him leave. In the final part of this book I want to outline some of the spiritual requirements worship leaders, musicians, singers and ministers should fulfil if we are to correctly handle and host the presence of God. Literally thousands of people have died through ignorance of how to handle God's holy presence. And though we have talked much through the pages of this book about God moving in glory upon our lives, we must acknowledge that an increase in God's glory means an increase in responsibility, especially from those called to lead.

Handling the Ark of His Presence

In the pages of the first book of Samuel, we find a remarkable series of events revolving around the Ark of the Covenant. The ark was, as you know, the gold-plated box God had commanded the Israelites to use as a symbol of his throne and promise. Above the ark were two cherubim (angelic beings). God had said to Moses, 'I will meet you there' between the outstretched wings of the cherubim (see Ex. 25:10–22).

Following the ark on its journey through a few stages of Israelite history, we can see how this symbol of God's presence impacted different circumstances. This story goes some way to teach us how to handle his glory in life and service.

Calling God's Presence 'It' – 1 Samuel 4

The children of Israel draw up battle lines against the Philistines, their arch-enemies. The first stage of the battle begins and the Israelites get badly beaten. Back at camp there is panic. A few desperate Israelites remember wars of old when they routed various large armies and dangers. Whole cities had fallen to the miraculous battle strategies of this fearsome tribe. Something had always been present in those battles: there had always been a common denominator, the ark of the covenant.

The Israelites said to themselves, 'Let us bring the ark of the covenant into the camp, that it may save us from our enemies.' I suppose they had a right to think it might save them – it had been present at many victories in the past, so they assumed it had a power of its own. They brought the ark into the camp, went out into battle, lost abysmally once again, and the ark was captured. At the same time a child was born called Ichabod, meaning 'the glory has departed'.

Let's learn from this: God gives us arks and other tools and symbols to help us. Things like worship leaders, worship styles, songs and PA systems. But please note the children of Israel said, 'It will save us', not 'He will save us'. While these things are not wrong in and of themselves, the moment we begin to rely on the 'its', and believe it is them that will save us, the presence of God departs. The day we depend on the 'arks' instead of on a personal relationship with God, the glory of God evacuates our lives.

It is amazing to watch the reaction of Christians who believe the way they always do things is the way they should be done. The songs, the music, the length of the meetings, the preaching style. Now while God gives us lovely things, if we depend on them rather than on him the glory will depart. If we depend on our 'three fast songs, three slow songs' formula, the glory and presence will run out of the door. Sadly, many might not know the difference when he has gone, and may keep on churning out the religious formula, however charismatic it may seem. But there will be no fire, no wind and no power to defeat the enemy.

Ron Kenoly wasn't playing in the background as Jericho fell; no Kendrick songs were being played when Jesus healed the sick. At the end of the day, you can live without all the 'its' if the power of God is with you. What is your attitude to the 'its' and arks he has given you? Are you more dependent on them and on your worship culture than on God? I had to overcome my dependence on the 'its' the day I found myself leading worship in the African bush, with no PA system, a guitar with three strings on it, and hundreds of people waiting for Spirit-led leadership.

As a worship leader you need to know, deeply, that God is with you. You need to know that you have a greater connection with his presence and power than with any of your 'tools', such as music, worship styles and culture. If you do not, his manifest presence probably left you a long time ago. You may not even be aware of it, as we can survive a long time on the 'its' – or at least until a crisis hits us!

God's Presence Among Other Gods –
1 Samuel 5:1–9

Once captured, the ark of God's presence was taken to Ashdod and placed in a pagan temple alongside other gods. In the morning the demonic god Dagon lay toppled before the ark. In a very short time an epidemic hit the land, with many covered in boils and tumours. They had made the dreadful mistake of thinking you could place our living God alongside other feeble excuses for divinity! No other god can ever stand beside the one true God for long.

And that includes the gods of our own worship ministries, plans and profiles. We don't want to be 'gods' alongside the true God. We want him to be revered and him alone. I know this is strong, pictorial language, but deep in the hearts of many performers there is the desire to be a 'god'. Pop and film stars are known as screen gods, or even, as the Beatles so notoriously did, equate themselves to Jesus.

It is sad to say, but many worship leaders would be just as much at home singing in a pub or club, trying to get into the charts or to become teen idols! There are, without a doubt, ego-issues in the hearts of most creative people that must be dealt with (mine certainly did). While desiring to have a song in the charts or give God a profile through fame is not wrong in itself, in worship ministry we must ensure our hearts are set on causing everyone to worship Jesus and Jesus alone. God once said to me, 'It's not your meeting or your platform – I just want you to give me a platform and let me have my meeting!' And that is the worship ministry – facilitating others to commune with Jesus, not with our gifting or good looks.

In scripture we find that as King Solomon's priests stepped down and got out of the way, God's glory invaded the temple. This is an important factor. Worship-leading is partly about stepping down and stepping aside, pointing people to God and getting out of the way. It's not about us pointing people to ourselves or getting our gifting to be seen.

I was once repeatedly invited to minister to a small group of people, an invitation that it took me a couple of years to fulfil. On reaching the meeting and setting up my keyboard, I sat down to play and lead worship. As soon as I started to play, God struck me dumb for over an hour! At first it was embarrassing, but then I realised everyone was having a great time without me, as the presence of God moved on people. I had to learn that

God can do things quite well without me. My ministry is not about putting on a good show, but about keeping out of God's way enough for him to touch lives as he wants to.

God's Presence Without the Blood – 1 Samuel 6:19–20

Let's return to our story: somewhat panicked by the epidemic and destruction of the gods, the Philistines sent the ark back to Israel and eventually it found its way to the men of Beth Shemesh. Intrigued by the ark, this small Israelite clan lifted the lid to look inside. Instantly seventy men died.

This is one of those unusual scriptures that leave you wondering what on earth has gone on. Why did God kill thousands of men merely for looking into the ark? Was he in a bad mood? Did he just get out of the wrong side of the bed that morning? To understand God's purpose here, you really need to understand the design of the ark of the covenant.

Inside the box-like ark were stored a few items, most notably the tablets of the Law (also called the Ten Commandments, which were the covenant or agreement made between the Israelites and God). The top of the box was a golden lid called 'the mercy seat'. Over the mercy seat, between the outstretched wings of the two cherubim, the supernatural glory of God would shine.

Once a year the high priest would enter into the most holy place in the tabernacle and sprinkle blood over the mercy seat. In effect, the priest would sprinkle blood between the glory of God (shining above between the cherubim) and the Law (hidden below inside the box). This meant that God would 'look down' from the glory between the cherubim, see the shed blood on the mercy seat and judge the people by the blood and not by the Law – the shed blood signifying that someone, or something, had taken the punishment for any acts committed that violated the Law.

What had the men of Beth Shemesh done by looking into the ark? They had lifted the mercy seat, thus removing the blood covering between the glory and the Law! This is one of the greatest lessons regarding God's presence: God's glory and holiness, without blood, will destroy you. The men of Beth Shemesh removed the blood that covered the Law, were instantly judged by that Law, were found wanting and instantly died.

Worship, presence, praise and glory are utterly painful without the blood of Jesus Christ. Feelings of guilt destroy worship time after worship time, causing us to run, hide and separate ourselves from him. No one can approach God without knowing the wonder of the shed blood of Jesus, his wonderful grace, mercy and love. We must enter the presence of God by the blood-stained way. A way you can't ever earn, but must receive through grace. A way whereby his sacrifice covers all our failures, even in the light of his intense holiness. We must always keep the mercy seat in place if we are to know his glory. If we fail to, he will 'kill us', as he is still the same holy God that he has always been.

When leading worship and hosting the presence of God in a meeting or in your life, always have an emphasis on the blood and sacrifice of Jesus. Always cause people to remember God's forgiveness and grace. When trying to come close to God, confess your sin and receive God's full forgiveness at the mercy seat. Then you can enjoy the pure intensity of his presence.

Never forget that God's presence is hosted by the blood of Jesus on the earth.

Imitating the World – 1 Chronicles 13

As we have already seen, after the ark had upset the Philistines, they sent it back to Israel. They did this by placing it on a new cart pulled by oxen and sending it on its way. There it was found by the men of Beth Shemesh, many of whom came to an untimely end.

After God killed the men of Beth Shemesh, the ark was stored in a house until, many years later, King David decided he wanted to bring it back to Jerusalem. Without really studying God's requirements for handling the presence, David tried to bring the ark into Jerusalem in the same way the Philistines had sent it – on a new cart. Now it might not seem like much to you or me, but David tried to handle God's presence in an inappropriate way, and a man called Uzzah died as a result. The ark rocked around a little as it was on its way, Uzzah reached out his hand to steady it and God killed him. Yet another story where you wonder if God was in a bad mood!

Of course, he wasn't. He just expected David to handle his holy presence with the respect he deserved. God had clearly outlined his requirement for handling the presence but David had ignored it. Reproved, David then delved into the scriptures and discovered that the ark was meant to be carried by Levitical priests, not new carts. On his next attempt to give the ark a home in Jerusalem, David was successful.

We can learn a very special lesson from this: because of apathy towards God's Law, David resorted to impersonating the world and the culture around him and simply assumed that what he had seen elsewhere, or heard about, was acceptable to God. He took hold of God's presence and treated it as the Philistines had, and God considered it sin enough to put a man to death. As we have seen elsewhere in this book, there is a definite right and wrong to worship. This cannot be ignored. We must discover God's blueprint.

Worship leader, you are not here to impersonate the world. You don't lead worship because you couldn't make it as a club singer. You are not in God's equivalent of *Top of the Pops* every Sunday. You're not here to show off, to perform or to entertain. You are here to respectfully host the presence of a living God, who could well kill you if you get it terribly wrong. Ask Ananias and Sapphira if you want a New Testament opinion (Acts 5)!

Learn how you should handle God's presence. Learn what your lifestyle should be like as a leader by studying the life of Jesus and the epistles. Live a life worthy of the calling you have received and don't for one short moment think you are on the platform because you have a right to perform. Not if you want to host the overwhelming presence of our king.

The presence of God is a fearsome thing. Handle his 'nearness' with grave honour and respect. Study hard, pray hard, and listen to God and the leadership he has given you. Worship in private as well as in public. Step aside and let God's presence be the focal point of those you are leading. Then you will have fulfilled the glorious challenge of hosting God's presence among his people.

The Challenge of the Chapter

- Thousands have died by incorrectly handling the presence of God.
- Don't replace God's presence with his gifts and 'tools' or programmes.

- Deal with any pride in your life, as Jesus must be the only one worshipped in your ministry.
- Do you remove God's mercy and slip into self-righteousness?
- Are you imitating the world in your worship ministry?

Chapter 14

PITCH YOUR TENT OF MEETING

Deep calls to deep in the roar of your waterfalls
All of your breakers have swept over me.
The longer I dwell near the whispers of your
*   heartbeat*
The more of your nature I'm finding in me.

Your Life Flows From Your Heart

'Keep thy heart with all diligence; for out of it are the issues of life'
(Prov. 4:23, KJV).

All the issues of your life flow from your heart. It is the spring from which all your attitudes, actions and desires stem. You are not a result of your circumstances, and neither are you the person your position or title says you are. You are who you truly are in your heart and in the secret place. No matter what you say or do, most people will see the real you eventually.

Many seek to lead worship and yet they do not have a heart after the presence of God. This is always obvious in their ministries, as you cannot pretend to have something you do not have. You cannot lead people in rapturous worship when you have no personal worship life. You cannot obey the Spirit in a meeting when you are rebellious to him outside the walls of the church. You cannot exemplify intimacy and tenderness of heart before the congregation when you haven't spoken to God all week. The only way God's presence is going to move in and around you is if you live a life soaked in his presence. Then you will be like a broken jar of perfume, with a presence flowing out of your heart. Everyone will see that you have been with Jesus.

Have You Pitched Your Tent?

During the time of Israel's wanderings in the desert, with the weeping and wailing of over 300 funerals a day and the noise of a million refugees and livestock, Moses took a tent and pitched it away from the hustle and bustle of the camp. There he would meet with God in power and glory, hearing God's voice and instruction (Ex. 33:7–11).

All of us need to pitch our tent of meeting away from the noise of life and ministry if we are to succeed in life, especially in worship ministry. There is no way we can avoid this spiritual necessity to spend time in God's presence and his word. The tent of meeting is a place of solitude where we hear his voice and our souls are restored. That tent of solitude becomes a tent of friendship, of grace, of glory and of revelation.

The Tent of Friendship

It was said of Moses that he and God spoke as friends at the tent of meeting. What a wonder: to speak with the Creator as a friend. Today the wonder of the New

Covenant is that we all know God, 'from the least to the greatest' (Heb. 8:11). No longer do we need high priests, or people to speak to God for us. Every one of us can know him as a friend, just as Moses did.

In 1990, God locked me into his presence for several months, when I found that all I could do was pray. He spoke to me over and over again, revealing to me my future, the things he wanted me to do, and how much he would care for me throughout my life. This time of friendship with God is one of the foundations of my whole life and ministry today, and is the reason why I find it easy to spend hours and days in his presence. He is my friend, and with a friend you can spend endless hours.

As we pitch our tent of meeting, by finding time and space to encounter God, our friendship with him will develop and grow. We will learn the deep things of God as he shares with us by his Spirit. If you wish to become a man or woman of God, you must pitch your tent of friendship away from the noise of modern-day life.

The Tent of Grace

Grace is the empowering of God, a favour that we don't deserve. But although we do not deserve his grace, that doesn't mean that we sit back and do nothing about it! God's grace doesn't come to the passive or apathetic. His grace is in a location and has to be searched for and found: 'Let us then approach the throne of grace with confidence, so that we may receive mercy and find grace . . .' (Heb. 4:16).

Empowering grace is found in the tent of meeting at the throne of God. If you want God to empower you for life and ministry, you need to come to the throne to find grace.

The prodigal son ran away from home and ended up in a pigsty. While he was sitting in the mud, his father's love was still certain and strong, and his father had much to give him and bless him with. But the father's love would not come to the pigsty to bless him there. The son had to go home, where his father's love could be found. He had to go to the place where that love could be experienced and expressed. God's love and empowering grace toward us are very much the same – he loves us all equally, but generally it is those who approach the throne of God who experience his empowering grace.

A short time ago, I found myself once again locked into God's presence, unable to leave. Here I found he was pouring unmerited favour, undeserved power and unearned mercy on me. Basking in his presence and soaking up all his goodness, I found that as I went out to minister, healings would happen before I could even touch people. God's presence filled the room where I stood. All because a feeble man like me can come to a throne called 'grace' and swim in God's river of mercy! If you swim, you'll get soaked; if you get soaked, you can splash a lot of other people!

It's time for a generation of people who know how to soak and swim in the grace of God at his throne, and carry that wondrous mercy to a hurting world. Come, then, to the tent of meeting and meet with God at the throne of grace.

The Tent of Glory

Moses experienced the glory of God at the tent of meeting. God would come down and trap Moses in the tent until he had finished speaking with him. Do you remember the old song?

> *Shut in with God in the secret place*
> *There by his Spirit beholding his face*
> *Gaining more power to run in the race*
> *I long to be shut in with God.*

Imagine the wonder of being shut in with God! Moses would come away, his face shining so brightly that he would have to cover his head because of the reflected glory. God stepped out of the invisible to be visibly seen by this humble man, such was his love for people who pitch a tent to seek his face.

As we seek to know God in the tent of meeting, we will know and reflect his glory. The more we soak in his presence, the more he will manifest his presence around us in our ministry. Signs and wonders will occur as a side-effect of our personally encountering his glory. Again and again I have noticed that the more time I spend in his presence, the more powerfully his presence manifests in services and the more powerful worship becomes. There is no shortcut to this place of power and glory – worship leaders must be worshippers in private as well as in public.

The Tent of Revelation

Finally, it is when we spend time in God's presence that he reveals his purposes and plans to us. In the tent of meeting God would speak to Moses again and again, instructing, advising and commanding him, giving him a daily plan for the lives of thousands of refugees. Such revelation will come to us today by the Spirit of God moving in and around us. It is as we hear him – the designer, draftsman and architect of the church – that a blueprint is found, a dwelling place for his glory is built and we lead the people of God with integrity, wisdom and power.

In the place of revelation we find not only God's general blueprint for right and wrong, but also his personal blueprint for our individual situations. There are demands and commands placed on my life that are not placed on yours, and vice versa, because of the specific purposes of our lives. These are found in the tent of revelation.

As we move into the final two chapters of this book, I want to look at the dynamic relationship between an individual and the Spirit of God, and the revelation he brings. How to hear his voice, find his blueprint and follow his guidance. This, more than any other teaching, has changed my life over the last ten years.

The Challenge of the Chapter

- Your ministry is a direct reflection of the state of your heart.
- Do you have a heart to seek after the glory of God?
- You cannot carry God's presence when you do not enjoy worship.
- Do you pray and worship in private often?

Chapter 15

THE HOLY SPIRIT IS THE WORSHIP LEADER

When you move, when you breathe
At your touch, I receive
At the kiss of your mouth
I tremble.

The best a leader can ever be in the kingdom of heaven is the first follower. Ultimately we are all followers of the Holy Spirit. No one can, and no one should, minister in any way other than under the unction of the Holy Spirit. He comes to clothe us in power, to give us wisdom and cause us to live at a supernatural level in our ministries.

Only the Spirit Can Fulfil God's Commands

Ezekiel 2:1–2 exemplifies an incredible truth about our need for the Holy Spirit. Ezekiel was lying face down before the glory of God when God spoke: 'He said to me, "Son of man, stand up on your feet and I will speak to you." As he spoke, the Spirit came into me and raised me to my feet, and I heard him speaking to me.'

God said to Ezekiel, 'Stand up', then the Holy Spirit came and stood him up. Ezekiel didn't fulfil God's command – God's Spirit did! Learn this liberating lesson now: you cannot fulfil God's commands, only God can. He gives you a job to do, then does it himself by the power of his Spirit in you. Receive this as a revelation: you cannot lead worship – the Holy Spirit is the only true worship leader.

From Filling to Following

Once we have been filled with the Holy Spirit we must follow him. When Jesus was filled with the Spirit at the Jordan (Lk. 3:22), he left that place and was 'led by the Spirit' from that day forward (Lk. 4:1).

Many people are *filled* with the Holy Spirit, but surprisingly few are *led* by the Spirit. This leads to a very frustrating kind of Christianity: you are filled with God, but you are doing nothing with that supernatural power. You are told that the God of the universe, who parted seas and destroyed nations, who is all-powerful and omniscient, is within you, yet your lifestyle is powerless and bland. You feel him moving around you, but do not understand what is required to cause his power to be released through you in ministry. This can lead to great disillusionment and disappointment. Once filled, you must discover how to follow the Spirit of God.

A Small, God-Connecting Moment

Moses stood at the Red Sea, full of God's power. But only when he did what God said, by raising his staff over the sea, did God's power part the sea and free the Children of Israel. This is the difference between being filled and being a follower. There is one small God-connecting moment when we do what we hear him command. In that instant we go from powerless religion to an electrifying relationship with God. It was the same even for Jesus. He said of himself: 'The Son can do nothing by himself; he can only do what he sees his Father doing' (Jn. 5:19).

A deaf and mute man was brought to Jesus in Mark 7:32. The Father showed him he should take the man away from the crowds, stick his fingers in his ears and spit on him! At that moment I would have started an argument with God and got the worship leader to sing a few loud songs!

But Jesus obeyed and the man was healed. Just one short God-connecting moment, when Jesus did what his Father said, and all of heaven came to earth for that deaf, mute man.

When Jesus ministered, he constantly listened to the Father and depended on the power of the Holy Spirit. He healed in many different ways: prayer, a word, a touch, spitting and even mudpacks. It wasn't that he was doing what he felt like, or wanted to be unconventional for the sake of it. He did unusual things because he was following his Father.

If the key to Jesus' success was communication with his Father, how much more do we need that communication in order to see God's power move? Imitation is not revelation. Mimicking, even mimicking the Bible's methods, is not good enough. We need to hear God moment by moment and fulfil those small, God-connecting instructions. It is the key to powerful Spirit-filled, Spirit-following leadership.

The Challenge of the Chapter

- You cannot lead worship, only the Holy Spirit can.
- Once filled with the Spirit, you must be led by the Spirit.
- Are you fulfilling God's personal instructions to you?
- When was the last time you stepped out to obey God and saw God's power move?

Chapter 16

HEARING THE VOICE OF GOD

I am like Ezekiel, lifted up to hear your voice
I am like Mary, afraid
I am like Daniel, my strength is gone, I
  cannot breathe
I lie like the elders at your throne
Lost in your glory, found in your love
Heart overwhelmed by the one that I love.

If we are going to lead worship in the power of the Holy Spirit, we must be able to hear God's voice. It is he who will tell us how to lead, what songs to sing, what ministry to engage in, and, very importantly, what *not* to do.

It is Your Right to Hear God

Many don't actually believe they have a right to hear God's voice. They presume we somehow were meant to muddle through life, hoping we are pleasing God. That's not the way the Bible states things should be: 'He who belongs to God hears what God says' (John 8:47).

If you belong to God, then you can and should hear his voice. It's your right to hear him moment by moment, day by day. He is ready to help and counsel you in all things. He wants to guide you in your preparations to lead worship and in your leadership during each meeting.

You Hear Him Already

What you must realise is that although you may say you don't hear God's voice, you actually hear him already. Let me prove it to you: how do you know you are saved? You just know, right? My dear friend Paul Gutteridge says that you know it in your 'knower'! How do you know when you've done something wrong? Once again, you just know it in your 'knower'. It's a spiritual thing. You can't chalk it on a blackboard or explain it easily, but in your spirit you know things.

Have you ever met someone you've never seen before and felt something about them – that they're good, or bad? It's the 'baby' stage of discernment. You're starting to listen to God and his Spirit at work in you. We have to take these simple beginnings of hearing and invest time in tuning our spiritual ears to hear God's voice, until we can hear him about specific things, using that sense of 'just knowing' in our 'knower'.

Faith for Hearing

Romans 12:6 tells us that we prophesy according to our faith. One meaning for that phrase is that we will prophesy (hear God and speak out) to the degree that we believe we can. In other words, if you don't think God can speak to you, you won't experience it. If you do, you will.

A while ago, I was ministering in a meeting when God pointed out a young couple and told me to prophesy over them. They were wonderful to prophesy to, because as I ministered to them they kept saying, 'Yes, yes, yes that's right!' The more they encouraged me that I was correct in my prophecies and words of knowledge, the more my faith grew, until I was becoming quite accurate in the things God was showing me for them.

As the prophecy continued I was talking about their daughter, how she looked, what God was saying to her, where she worked etc. I was full of faith and hearing God according to the measure of my faith, which was increasing all the time! Then it happened: God said to me, 'And her name is . . .' Suddenly fear gripped me. I screeched to a halt and I said to God quietly, 'Lord, you can tell me what she looks like: there are only a few different hair colours. You can tell me where she might work: there's a one-in-a-hundred chance of getting it right. But Lord, her name: that's one chance in thousands! I could blow it all!' I turned to the couple and said, 'What's her name?' Of course it was the name I had thought and heard. By then, though, it was pointless for me to share that fact!

Fear had paralysed me and immediately cut off my ability to hear. Why? Because I believed I could hear about how someone looked, or what someone did, but I didn't believe I could hear someone's name. You will hear God to the measure that you believe you will hear God. How much do you believe you can hear God right now?

Develop Sensitivity

In order to grow in our ability to follow the Spirit, we must develop our faith and sensitivity. I spend time most days with a pad and a pen, listening to the voice of God. I sit down, pen in hand, and just start to write what I think God might be saying to me. Irreverent, you might think, but actually, if you think that you have God's Spirit inside you to the extent that, as the Bible says, you are 'one spirit with him', then it is no wonder that God's wisdom is stirring in your life.

I started doing this in 1990 on the instruction of a wonderful man of God. It actually played a large part in the birth of my ministry, as for several months I spent four hours a day writing down what God was saying to me regarding my future.

Not only that, but I began to share with other people things God was saying to me about them. I think I was more amazed than them at how accurate some things were! That's when I realised hearing God's voice is meant to be a natural part of our daily walk.

I'd encourage you to sit down and start to develop your sensitivity to God's voice every day if you want to lead God's people. Simply start to write down what you think God might be saying to you. Ask questions and write down what you think he is saying. Stretch your faith. Be bold! Don't sit around waiting for a great booming voice. God doesn't speak with an audible voice too often. I've only heard his voice audibly a couple of times in thirty years. Most of the time it's just a feeling – a knowing – deep down. I sometimes call it a 'peace-filled hunch'. The more I go with that 'peace-filled hunch' and listen to God, the more I hear.

How do You Know it's God?

Of course, that doesn't mean that everything you hear, think or feel is from God. Part of our practice of developing sensitivity is to learn what is of God and what is not. Here are five basic tests to see whether what you are hearing is from God.

1. **Does it display the fruit of the Spirit?** (Mt. 7:15–20 and Gal. 5:22–23.) Does it have the nature of God? It should be loving, kind, compassionate, even if it has some discipline included.
2. **Does it give God the glory?** (1 Jn. 4:2–3.) Does it glorify Jesus as Lord, or someone else (e.g. is it hugely self-centred)?
3. **Does it submit to the counsel of many?** (Jas. 3:17.) Is there anyone mature who can confirm the word?
4. **Does it draw you to Jesus?** (Jn. 16:15.) Anything that is of God will draw you towards him in ever-deepening relationship.
5. **Does it line up with the word?** (Titus 2:1.) Does it line up with the nature and character of God displayed in the word of God?

Develop your sensitivity to God's voice and you will discover the greatest tool available to you as a leader and a Christian. Without God's voice we are like people walking in darkness. In that dark land the Bible is nothing more than a set of rules we are trying to keep in order to serve God. That has never been God's plan for us and never will be. His passion is for an intimate relationship of love, communion and communication.

Hearing his voice will connect you with his power and purpose for your life. By hearing and obeying, you will release his glory into your meetings and worship times. Every time you submit to that small, God-connecting command, no matter how simple it is, God's purposes will be released and you will be walking in the Spirit instead of in imitation or liturgy. This is where the adventure begins!

The Challenge of the Chapter

- It is your daily right to hear God's voice.
- You have already heard his voice often, even if you don't recognise it.
- You will only hear God as much as you believe you can.
- If you do not hear God's voice, you cannot obey him and will not see his power at work.
- Are you daily developing your sensitivity to God's voice?

Chapter 17

EIGHT 'MUST-HAVES' FOR GLORY IN YOUR CHURCH

Aching, crying, a world of hurt
Groaning, creation awaits your word
Your sons, your Church shall be revealed
Favour and glory as a shield
Begin with us . . .
Would you come and rest your glory in this place?

We're approaching the end of our time together now, and my mind is drawn to an email I received a few years ago. I had spent several days teaching all the truths outlined in this book, and then experiencing something of God's glory with the gathered church in rural South Africa. I left on Easter Sunday and the church gathered once again to meet God. Several days later I received this email from John Gardiner, then editor of South Africa's most successful Christian magazine:

'On Easter Sunday the presence of the Lord was so strong that the entire church were lying face down in the dust (they meet in a tent). They have a number of illegal bars in the area, and they became aware that all the activity and noise had stopped in these places – and when they looked out, the people in the bars were also lying face-down towards the church meeting place!'

The glory of God had hit the church, then spilled out into the illegal bars around it. The illegal bars (called 'Shebeens'), where locals take drugs, get drunk and find prostitutes, became a runway for God's glory and he knocked them off their seats!

But what can you do, as a worship leader or pastor, to bring these greater levels of glory into your church? Here are eight 'must-haves' if you are seeking to increase God's presence in your church:

Must-Have No. 1: A Clear Common Vision

One of the greatest areas of conflict in any church is often found in the worship team. This is perhaps due to the fact that many creative people are a little insecure (myself included!), but in the main it comes when the worship leaders have one vision for worship, while the senior leader has another.

I get many letters and emails from frustrated worship leaders who are longing to see God's glory break out in their churches, sometimes in situations where there is no desire in the senior leaders for this to take place.

The bottom line is that the vision of the church flows from the top, down. A longing for glory is no excuse for rebellion, unrest and conflict. A senior leader really needs to have a desire to build a church filled with glory, in order for anything of that nature to take place in the worship team or congregation.

Many churches these days are very content to use a 'four fast songs, three slow songs' model for worship, preach the word and engage in social action. Sadly, the power of the presence, miracles and healings are often missing in these places.

But when a pastor longs for glory, a worship team hunger for presence, and a congregation rise up to seek God's face, miraculous moments like those in South Africa can take place. I have been in churches where bodies lay in the street, such is the presence of God; where people in wheelchairs get up and dance as God's presence arrives; where the unsaved ask, 'What must I do to be saved?' after falling to the floor under God's power. All because the leaders, band and congregation are hungry for the same thing.

Worship leader – align yourself with your pastor's vision. Gain a place of influence by being servant-hearted. Pray, discuss, give them this book – anything to spark new ideas of a greater future in their hearts. Most of all, submit to a gradual process towards more glory in your church. Remember, your pastor has much more to think about than just the worship culture of your church, so do be patient.

Pastors – seek God about your church. How does it line up against the glory-filled church in the book of Acts? Have you stepped back from the big vision of seeking God for miracles, because the slick, concert-imitating, social-orientated church is easier to build? Have you been tricked into thinking that yours is the only model that can bring in the 'numbers'? In actual fact, millions of unsaved people are waiting for the true, supernatural church to arise. Our own church grew by over 60 per cent in eighteen months as we increased our search for God's glory. See if you can find some way, without discrediting other areas of vision, for presence to increase in your church.

Must-Have No. 2: A Place to Adventure

In real, local church life, there are many things that need to happen: baby dedications, announcements, presentations, communion, pastoring and a clear preaching of the word of God. In my own church we recognise the need for basic church necessities: Sunday school, care for people, teaching, organisational and legal commitments . . . the list goes on!

So I recommend that, in our busy church life, we find a safe place, a home for adventure and experimentation; a place where seeking God's glory is the priority. Some pastors try to do this in Sunday morning services, but they can be the hardest place for this. There's often an 'expectation' on Sunday mornings that works against thoroughly relaxing and trying new things.

We have found that our places of experimentation and adventure are Sunday evenings, home groups and conferences. If you were to come to our church on a Sunday morning you might well think we're a pretty normal charismatic church. Our two morning services last a little over one hour, are pretty 'shallow', fun and family-orientated.

But if you came to the evening (which we call 'Deeper'), you would find we don't watch the clock. The meetings can go on for hours, with worship, ministry, teaching and powerful moves of the Spirit. The presence of God is evident, miracles take place and new things are experienced. It's our place to adventure.

Where is your place to adventure? It may be Sunday evenings like ours, or once a month on a Saturday night? It could be a mid-week evening or a home-based group. It all depends on your church size, busyness and even the specific gifting of your leadership.

I have found that growing a church in glory doesn't always have to mean removing musicians and confronting whole congregations, as I did in 1993. It can be just as powerful to start in a home with a passionate group, moving to a monthly main meeting as things develop. Eventually, you can build up to a weekly place of adventure with a large percentage of your church involved. I dream that one day, like the early church, we will have a daily place of adventure, with God's Spirit rushing through the church like a mighty wind.

We have found that, over time, the freedom of our adventure meetings begins to spill over into all the other meetings, and the supernatural begins to flow through the whole church. I've even found our Sunday school children flat out on their backs, being filled with God's presence and hearing his voice!

Rather than confront your whole church with a brave vision of the supernatural, why not find a place to adventure? Gather a small group who are passionate, and begin a journey that will ultimately affect your whole congregation.

Must-Have No. 3: L-Plates

In England, learner drivers have to attach L-plates to their cars to signify to others their inexperience. I can vividly remember, in my juvenile pride, longing to rip them off so I could no longer be identified as a beginner. I longed to look experienced!

I spend much of my time in church encouraging people to put their spiritual L-plates back on. We need to be open about the fact that we are learning and real about the mistakes we make. As long as we seek to love and serve, no great harm can be done.

Once again, I prefer to have a set place where experimentation and adventure take place, aside from our larger Sunday morning services. A safe zone where we can all learn together. The prophetic, the miraculous and free worship are often discredited by inexperienced learners trying hard to be Spirit-led and barraging headlong into main services with disastrous results. This does so much to harm the moving of the Spirit and the rising desire for more supernatural in the hearts of the congregation.

Creating safe zones of learning enables worship leaders, pastors and congregation members to learn how to bring prophetic songs, prophecies, pray for the sick, think creatively and engage in new worship expressions. Once we learn what works for us, this can easily spill over into other areas of church life, with little harm done.

For this reason we also encourage prophetic song, musicianship and experimentation in our worship practises. If a band can't do things in a practise time, then never ask them to try in main services, as the result will only discredit the band, or even worse, the Holy Spirit.

Must Have No. 4: Leadership, Not Self-Indulgence

There are some misapprehensions about Spirit-led worship that I do not want to be accused of causing.

Some worship leaders and musicians can make classic mistakes, feeling that worship that goes on for a long time is spiritual. Some prophetic songs seem to last for hours, as a singer doesn't know when to stop. Musicians can close their eyes and get lost in a cool groove, believing that because a thing is spontaneous, it is prophetic. It is important to note that not everything that is spontaneous is prophetic, just as not everything that is well-practised is flesh.

One of the most common failings of so-called 'prophetic' worship bands, is to be entranced in the music, while the whole congregation stands watching – at best entertained, at worst bored. That is only marginally closer to Spirit-led worship than a worship leader who is tied to their song list. Spirit-led worship leaders must follow God, but also draw people to God. If no one is following you, then your worship is self-indulgent and not leadership at all.

Always lead with your eyes open. Always have one eye on God and the other on the people (but do avoid looking cross eyed!). Serve God and serve people. There's a huge difference between serving God with your gifting and being servant-hearted. Make sure your servant heart is gently leading people from where they're at, to the throne room of God.

Must-Have No. 5: Excellence, Not Perfection

Now the reality is you won't always get to the throne room! You might be all fired up, passionate about God and ready for deep, glorious encounters but sometimes your people are simply not prepared to go there. In any congregation, some may be depressed, angry, backslidden, sick, lonely, inexperienced or tired. You can do all you can do, but you cannot force worship.

With this in mind, be excellent, but realise there is no perfect worship 'Utopia' out there. I love worship. I have worship leaders that love the presence of God and we have a congregation that love to worship but we still have varying levels of presence in any meeting. It's always down to the hearts of the people.

So I take the pressure off our worship leaders. They'll often come to me before a service and say, 'What shall I do?' I reply, 'Whatever.' Sometimes they may be a bit nervous, out of sorts or tired themselves. I simply say, 'Relax – let's enjoy this journey. If worship lasts five minutes, fine; if it last two hours, fine. There's no pressure on you to usher heaven to earth. That's everybody's job!'

I find the more relaxed everyone is, the more powerful worship becomes. Get rid of perfectionism and start enjoying life. Let glory flow through your church like waves and tides. Sometimes deep, sometimes loud, sometimes shallow, sometimes soft. God will bring a glorious fresh difference to every service, if we simply let God be God.

Must-Have No. 6: Wage War on Boredom

Some leaders say, 'Don't have change for change's sake.' I beg to differ! Change is good: it keeps us supple; it keeps us alive. If you want to keep people out of religion and engaged with God, you need to wage a war on boredom.

A beautiful aquarium opened in our city of Hull a few years ago and I went along to see the sharks. It was amazing to see these terrifying creatures close up. They looked at you as if to say, 'If it wasn't for this glass, you'd be lunch, chum!' Vicky and I took out an annual membership so we could visit at will. However, as the months went on we noticed the sharks slowly becoming more and more inactive, until they actually looked quite bored. After a year, their eyes seemed to yawn, 'Oh it's you again.'

Church leaders have to do all they can to demolish the 'Yawn . . . It's you again' feeling our churches can so often fall into.

In our adventure meetings I often change around the seating. I turn them around to face the back, bring all the seats onto the platform or even take them all away. I make sure worship times last different lengths, I mess up how we do communion, I use language outside of our own spiritual culture and I let my congregation hear leaders from other denominations and streams. I love to hold workshops when people think it's a teaching time, to sing when we should be hearing a preacher, minister when we normally sing, joke when it's quiet and go deeper when some want to stop.

They say there are two types of people in the world: those who have heart attacks and those who cause them. Which are you?

Must-Have No. 7: Friends to Inspire You

When it comes to change, it takes creativity and ideas. While I know much of this comes directly from the throne room of God, as we encounter him, God has also given us each other to inspire us and make us think.

I changed radically when I heard my friend and prayer minstrel Godfrey Birtill lead worship (actually prayers in song) for the first time. He made all sorts of noises as he sang, brought songs you could hardly sing and followed God's Spirit against all church culture. But there's an awesome presence around him. At one of our conferences, as he led people felt God's presence as they passed by in cars outside.

I have many friends who inspire me, challenge me and release me from my own religiosity (please don't tell me you're not religious – I don't believe you!). I also attend conferences where different things are taking place – things that stretch my mindset and practices.

Many people also travel to our events, where they experience God in new, deep ways. We always have a stream of letters after our annual Prophetic Worship Conferences and Encounter Conferences telling of worship leaders still drunk in the Spirit days later, remarkable worship times taking place and new gifts and new ideas pouring into church life. That inspiration is worth more than gold in local church life.

Do your utmost to find friends that want the same thing and dig for the gold of inspiration.

Must-Have No 8: Lots and Lots of the Holy Spirit

Finally, and most importantly – if you do none of the above, make sure you do this – have lots and lots of the Holy Spirit in your life, in your church and in your meetings.

Ephesians 3:19 tells us we can 'be filled to the measure of all the fullness of God'. That's an amazing amount of fullness! You can be filled to what measure? The measure of the fullness of God.

He is your creativity, he is the worship leader, he is the prophetic Spirit, the miracle-worker, the one who warms hearts and the one who leads meetings.

Every day, in every meeting, in every worship practise, in every possible way, ask for God to fill you with his Spirit. Get your people to look heavenward, that your worship would be an encounter and not a song service, a supernatural embrace of divinity and humanity, a kiss of honour against the cheek of an invisible Saviour.

If you have the Spirit, you will have all you need. So be drenched, overwhelmed, overcome and under-girded with him. You will never and can never be the same again.

The Challenge of the Chapter

- Do the worship team and the senior church leader share the same vision for worship?
- Do you have a place to adventure in God?
- Is there a learning culture at your church?
- Are you actively seeking ways to combat boredom?
- Are you desperately seeking the Holy Spirit in your life?

Epilogue

THE CHURCH OF THE FUTURE

> *When there's thousands filling stadiums*
> *Your glory falling down like rain*
> *The blind are seeing, the lame are walking*
> *The mute tongue singing, the dead are raised*
> *When the rulers of the nations*
> *All cry out 'How can I be saved?'*
> *Then the days of wonder are upon us.*

And so we come to the end of our time together. We have laughed at ourselves, at our shallowness at times, and at our need for more of God. We have groaned at our imitation and lack of authenticity. We have considered what we do in church and discovered that though most is sincere, perhaps not all is quite what God would have for us. There must be a new wineskin, supple and ready to receive new wine from heaven.

We have looked at our blueprint for worship, and talked much about the Spirit of God, the glory of God, and God's desire to fill our meetings, homes and prayer lives with his power. This is, of course, in order that we may see his glory in the workplace, among our neighbours and on the streets, so that thousands may come to a knowledge of Christ.

As I write, our way of life is threatened by terrorism and fear. Spirituality and the supernatural are of increasing interest to a western world that realises science and government have not brought about the Utopia it had hoped for. Now, more than ever, there is the opportunity for the church to shine as a refuge in a hurting world. Now is the time for her to arise in glory and impact a fearful and frightened world with the one truth and kingdom that will not fail: the Gospel of Jesus Christ, revealed through Spirit-empowered preaching and accompanied by signs, wonders and the miraculous.

But what exactly will that new wine, that glory, look like? I am quite sure that without a vision we will indeed perish, and so we must have some idea from heaven, from God himself, of what the church of the future will be like. We have hinted at many things in this book – but let me give you a vision of church given me by God some years ago.

In 1996 I encountered the glory of God in a six-week visit to South Africa. In that time I was filled with a vision for the United Kingdom and Europe. Night after night I awoke, day after day I prayed, and visions of a great revival were burned into my heart. I am convinced the church must be ready to host a glory revealed at a level previously unknown.

The presence of God is preparing to sweep across Europe as never before. It will be in response, as I have already shared in my first chapter, to the apostolic reformation currently underway. Stadiums, arenas and the greatest auditoriums will be turned into church buildings. Market places filled with thousands will be overcome by the glory of God. The blind will see. The lame will walk. Street evangelism will happen as never seen before, as mass healings take place on street corners and in shopping centres. Where many have spent years sowing, others will reap on a massive scale.

God's glory will touch the media, politics and royalty. His glory will invade live TV shows, as men and women of God reveal the power of God in healings, strange signs and prophetic words and wisdom. Many politicians will come to Christ in a very visible way. For some this will bring prominence, for others ridicule and scandal. Governments and kings will call days of prayer.

Thousands will stream into the kingdom of God as a great move of signs and wonders floods our churches, workplaces and homes. Some believers will be transfigured as Moses was. Trances, dreams and visions will become commonplace. The weather will be controlled by believers at certain times, and used as a sign to communities where they are ministering. Neighbours will knock on the doors of those known to be Christians, begging to be led to Christ and to find peace for their souls. Many businesses and workplaces will hold prayer meetings; some will even close for whole days of prayer. Study groups will meet at all hours of the day in business establishments.

The glory of God will fill the greatest auditoriums in the land as Christians try to find meeting places that can contain the numbers flooding into the kingdom. Great and glorious signs and wonders will be performed by apostolic teams, though even the least among the church will see miracles as commonplace. Churches will be planted on a daily basis. Leaders will be trained quickly and released easily. Youngsters will lead churches of hundreds and thousands. A softening of hearts between generations in churches will mean all ages will worship and walk together.

And Worship Ministry in the Church of the Future?

In the coming move of God's glory in the earth, worship ministry will change greatly, not so much because of our own skill and design but because men and women will be so overwhelmed by the presence of God. At times, whole bands will physically collapse under the weight of his presence. On occasions, crowds will stream out of auditoriums, terrified as God's glory is revealed in clouds, 'writings on the wall' (Daniel 5), earthquakes, audible voices and manifestations of angelic beings.

In local churches, many congregations will worship and sing without formal worship/music ministries. There will simply be too many Christians to be served by musical bands. People will meet from house to house, where spontaneous worship will flow on, led by the Spirit himself. Singing in tongues and intercessions will last for hours and days at a time. Leaders will often take a back seat and let God lead his people, trusting the intensity of his holiness and presence to keep the meetings in some sense of heavenly 'order'. The revival will be known as a 'leaderless' one in many places, as the glory of God will rest on the corporate church rather than on just a few prominent figures.

Every expression of worship, from extravagant foolishness to tender quietness, will flow like waves through churches. Denominational barriers, styles and wrong authority structures will break down in many communities and countries, leaving the church full of variety and flavour but without barriers and comparison.

Wonderful worship bands, anointed to facilitate God's presence and move in the prophetic, will be raised up. Albums that seem to capture the very intensity of God's presence will be used to impact millions. Radio and TV will open up to Christian music and feature glorious worship times with signs and wonders. These broadcasts will impact many households, and through the medium of TV millions will be saved, experiencing the presence of God in worship.

Some communities will feature 24-hour worship times, lasting for months and even years. Some of these will become incredible hot spots of God's glory, and the light of God's presence will be physically seen from miles around at times. Many people, saved and unsaved, will be overwhelmed by God's Spirit when attempting to travel near these places. There will be 100 per cent success rates in praying for the sick in some of these communities, a fact that will result in thousands visiting for prayer. Kings and presidents will visit them and find their hearts melting, touched by the glory of God during worship.

What Will You Do?

As you can see, I believe extraordinary days are ahead of us. What will you do to redesign your corporate worship, church, ministry and lifestyle for the glory of God? In some way, the glories outlined above depend on the preparation of your church temple. This is a biblical truth.

Will you stand on the sidelines while others pioneer new blueprints for the corporate gathering capable of bending to the weight of God's glory? Will you look at your life and ask yourself: 'Where can I follow God more, be filled with him more and show his glory more?' Will you look at your worship ministry and honestly examine the validity of its origins? Is it man-made, or God-made? If it is God-made, is it a relic of a past move, or is it a fresh design, the ink still wet from the master's pen?

Gather your leaders and ask God together, 'Lord, what must we do to host your glory? What is your specific worship blueprint for us?' I am quite sure he will answer, whether by word or by circumstances. And on that day you will begin a journey to build a temple for his presence in the earth. And who knows what will happen on the day God's awesome glory fills that temple?

ABOUT THE DAYS OF WONDER TRUST

The Days of Wonder Trust is a missions and media ministry operating out of the New Life Church, Kingston upon Hull. Since 1997 the Days of Wonder team have been involved in various ventures including:

World Missions
Jarrod and the team have ministered in over twenty nations in short- and long-term missions, raising churches to new levels of the power and presence of God. New Life Church is also the home of Colombia ChildCare UK, feeding, clothing, educating and bringing the Gospel to over 1,500 of the poorest children of Colombia each day. For further information visit www.cccuk.org

Events
Days of Wonder conducts worship events around the world, as well as three annual conferences in Kingston upon Hull: a prophetic worship conference, church conference and women's conference. Visit www.daysofwonder.org.uk for further information.

Television
Our 30-minute television programme Days of Wonder features great music, teaching and inspiration, with Jarrod and special guests.
Visit www.daysofwonder.org.uk for latest schedule.

Radio
The Days of Wonder radio show is a 30-minute teaching time with Jarrod, broadcast on FM, SKY Digital, NTL and on-line globally. There is also a 24-hour worship radio station on-line at www.daysofwonder.org.uk

For further information
visit www.daysofwonder.org.uk

KING OF KINGS, MAJESTY
JARROD COOPER

King of Kings, Majesty

King of Kings, Majesty features Jarrod's best and most loved songs, penned over ten years. Released by Authentic Music and recorded around the UK and in Nashville, this is an ideal album to encounter God with.

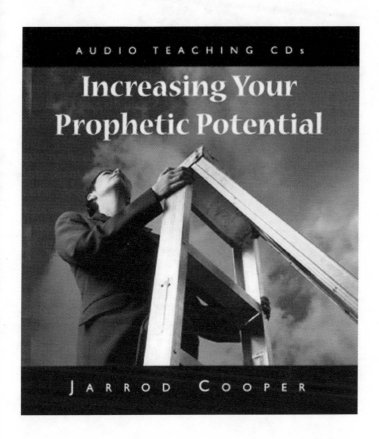

Increasing Your Prophetic Potential

A DVD/Audio teaching set featuring dynamic instruction on growing in the prophetic. Guaranteed to make you laugh, long and learn, this set will teach you how to hear God's voice, interpret what he is saying and minister it to others.

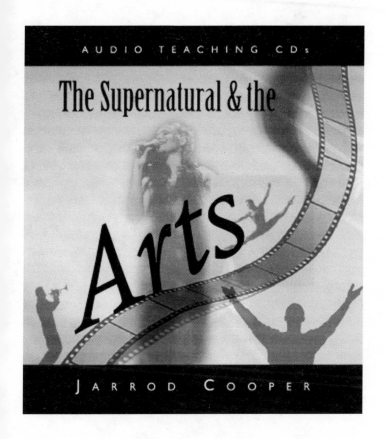

The Supernatural and the Arts

A series of four messages on CD from Kensington Temple's Summer School of the Arts, where Jarrod teaches how creativity and the supernatural were made to move hand in hand.